# Hunt, Point, Retrieve Dogs, for Work and Showing

# Hunt, Point, Retrieve Dogs, for Work and Showing

### N.C.DEAR

THE CROWOOD PRESS

First published in 2009 by
The Crowood Press Ltd
Ramsbury, Marlborough
Wiltshire SN8 2HR

enquiries@crowood.com
www.crowood.com

Revised edition 2024

**British Library Cataloguing-in-Publication Data**
A catalogue record for this book is available from the British Library.

ISBN 978 0 7198 4444 7

**Illustration credits**
The line drawings were prepared by Rebecca Dockeray. All photographs are by the author unless othrwise stated.

**Disclaimer**
The author and the publisher do not accept any responsibility, or liability, in any manner whatsoever, for any error or omission, or any loss, damage, injury, or adverse outcome of any kind incurred as a result of the use of any of the information contained in this book, or reliance upon it. If in doubt about any aspect of choosing, owning, showing, training, or working any breed of HPR dog, or entering them for field trials and working tests, readers are advised to seek professional advice.

Typeset by Magenta Publishing Ltd
Printed and bound in India by Nutech Print Services

**About the Author**
The author has been working with dogs since the mid-1980s – his first dogs were Irish Setters. The arrival of a Hungarian Vizsla in 2003 heralded the move to the HPR group of gundogs with success in Field Trials and Working Tests and is an A Panel Field Trial Judge. As well as other Vizslas, he also owned and worked a German Shorthaired Pointer.

He was the Field Trial Secretary for the Hungarian Vizsla Society prior to employment at The Royal Kennel Club as Field Trial Secretary for nearly 10 years.

He enjoys working and picking-up at a local shoot and is Chairman of the Hungarian Vizsla Society

# Contents

*The Brittany has a fast hunting style, and is a keen game finder.*

# Preface to the 2nd Edition

As a complete beginner in the HPR world everything was strange. I struggled with the fundamentals of training a dog to the level necessary to compete in Working Tests and Field Trials. My long-suffering trainers – dauntingly successful themselves, and blunt northerners – endured my incompetence with thinly disguised frustration. But we all persevered, and slowly but surely progress was made. Consistent failures at Working Tests gradually turned into consistent successes, and a similar pattern followed when entering the scary Field Trials.

During this time, I sought other sources of information – books – that I could digest at leisure away from the training field. I found that there were few texts dedicated to the HPR and that they were written by experts in the field. Some were simply out of date and/or out of touch with the times. They did not tell me what I wanted to know: things so basic that the experts took for granted and didn't think they were worth writing about. After all, everyone knows that. Don't they?

It dawned on me that if I could not find a book that 'spoke' to me, at my basic level, then maybe I should write it. Some thought it arrogant that a beginner, not into the game for 5 minutes should have the audacity to author a book! I thought it made complete sense. After all, I now knew more than before, not exactly a beginner but far from being an experienced hand.

I hope, therefore, that as a questioning beginner, the reader will find some of the answers within these pages.

Nigel Dear
March 2024

*The Italian spinone's slow trotting gait allows it to hunt large areas.*

# Introduction

When you first consider acquiring a hunt, point, retrieve dog it is unlikely that you will have any idea of where this might take you. What was first thought of as a pet suddenly transforms into a passport to the show ring, the shooting field, to gundog training and the working test. The world of field trials opens up to you. This is what happened to the author, who first caught sight of a beautifully elegant dog standing on the back of a Range Rover at the local clay pigeon shooting ground. Enquiring within as to what this was, he then set off on the trail, which resulted in the addition of a Hungarian Vizsla to the household. One thing leads to another: gundog training followed, the world of working tests and field trials beckoned, with success in the latter leading to Crufts and the show ring. All this, from one dog!

While learning the ropes at ringcraft, struggling with the gundog training, wondering whether we would be capable of competing at working tests, and with no knowledge of any of the tests themselves, it became apparent that there was no reference available to help the beginner in understanding the wide and fascinating world of the HPR dog: hence this book. This is the first comprehensive guide to the world of the HPR: showing, how to train your gundog, working tests with the actual tests being described in detail for the first time, and how to compete in field trials. This most demanding of the field disciplines – often a mystery and daunting to the beginner – is described, with tips on how to manage your runs successfully, and avoid the many pitfalls. So it is hoped that in demystifying the unknown, the reader will be encouraged to take the plunge, join a training class, and start their own journey in show and working tests, in spring pointing or field trialling, in any one or all of them. It is all there for you and your HPR dog.

# Chapter 1

# The HPR Dog

The hunt, point, retrieve breeds comprise a recognized sub-group of gundog, which, as the description suggests, are able to perform all three gundog tasks, thereby differentiating them from retrievers that retrieve, pointers and setters that hunt and point but do not retrieve, and spaniels that hunt and retrieve but don't point. As an all-rounder, the HPR is regarded as an all-purpose gundog. Bred originally for use on the shooting field, all the HPR breeds are now popular as pets and in the show ring.

All the HPR breeds make excellent family companions in the right home, but they need a lot of exercise (see sidebar, below), and they will need training. All HPRs can be trained to a very high standard, well beyond that required for a family pet, but it does not mean that they are all easy to train. Breeding has a big part to play in how the dog will behave – a dog from a very strong working strain, bred to do field work, may well be beyond the capabilities of the average person to train successfully, since it

needs the specialist knowledge and dedication of those who use these dogs for working. But don't be put off, there will be one for you if you take the time to choose carefully. There is more information on this subject in Chapter 3, 'How to Choose your HPR'.

## DEVELOPMENT OF THE HUNT, POINT, RETRIEVE DOG

As the gun gained currency as the hunter's weapon of choice, and with the emergence of the shotgun, there was a growing requirement for a dog that could range in front of him in search of game. As the hunter at that time only had what was available, the dogs of the time were encouraged to work in a manner that assisted the walking gun. Some turned out to be totally unsuitable, but others that showed something of ability were bred and cross-bred to produce animals in which the desirable attributes are now instinctive and natural. With the basis of the breed in place, breeding programmes became more formalized and concentrated. In Germany, for example, the German shorthaired, longhaired and wirehaired pointers followed highly controlled breeding programmes to ensure that only the best stock was used in order to protect the development of the breed, a policy that continues today. In Hungary, the Hungarian Vizsla was so prized that it could only be kept by the aristocracy, who continued to breed it very carefully.

If you are considering acquiring an HPR as a pet, a word of caution: while all the HPR breeds can make lovely family companions, they are energetic and intelligent, and need lots of exercise daily. They are not dogs to be left at home for long periods: intelligent dogs become bored quickly and this can, and often does, lead to them becoming destructive in the home. Lack of exercise will result in an out-of-condition, irritable and unhappy dog. If you cannot be at home with them during the day, or are not able to take them with you and to exercise them during the day, please do not get one.

*A Slovakian rough-haired pointer.*

In the UK, HPR dogs are used for hunting game birds such as pheasant, partridge, woodcock, snipe and grouse, to a lesser extent ground game such as hare and rabbit, and for working with falcons and hawks, and with the deerstalker as well as with the rough shooter. In their native countries they are also used for tracking deer or wild boar. In the home or in the show ring, the HPR breeds continue to grow in popularity; they are seen in increasing numbers in the agility discipline, which suits their energetic character.

# Chapter 2

# The HPR Breeds

There are nine HPR breeds currently in the UK that can be considered as established in the field and in the show ring, all of which are recognized by the Kennel Club; these breeds are described in this chapter. There are others, such as the Slovakian rough-haired pointer, the Korthals Griffon, the Pudelpointer, the Bracco Italiano and the Braque d'Auvergne (popular in the Czech Republic but virtually unknown in the UK), but these are not covered in this book because they currently exist in such small numbers that it is unlikely you will come across them.

## BRITTANY

The Brittany originated in the Callac region of France, appearing as a result of matings between the local fougère and the English pointers and setters owned by the English gentry who visited the region for partridge and snipe shooting. Often confused with the spaniel, to which it is similar in appearance, the Brittany is highly spirited with a fast hunting style, a keen game finder, and with a growing following amongst falconers and the rough shooter.

*The Brittany.*

*German longhaired pointer.*

## GERMAN LONGHAIRED POINTER

The German longhaired pointer developed as a result of the need for a faster, wider-ranging dog than the typical fowling dog used by hunters in Germany in the early nineteenth century. Crossing with the English setter resulted in a much faster dog that fulfilled this need. The breed standard was formalized in 1878–9, and subsequent breeding concentrated on improving the dog's hunting abilities. A relatively recent introduction to the UK, the breed was recognized by the Kennel Club in 2007.

A relatively large dog, undocked due to the protective nature of the long coat, it is an extremely enthusiastic hunter, able to work tirelessly, and which characteristically quarters energetically, this relative newcomer is gaining in popularity and establishing itself in the field.

*German shorthaired pointer.*

## GERMAN SHORTHAIRED POINTER

Numerically the most popular and arguably the most successful of the HPR breeds, the German shorthaired pointer was developed in the early nineteenth century in Germany as an all-purpose gundog. A medium-sized dog with a short coat, and traditionally docked, it is a keen game finder and an ideal shooting companion for the rough shooter. The origin of the German shorthaired pointer is not clear, as with most of the breeds, but the foundation stock was probably the German bird dog, related to the old Spanish pointer, and various crossings with local German scent hounds and tracking dogs (Schweisshunde). English pointers were introduced to lend elegance, resulting in a highly capable gundog with good looks and a very even temperament. The German shorthaired pointer can be spectacular to watch: it is very fast and wide-ranging in its work, and has excellent hunting capabilities, all of which have made it the dog of choice for many a field trialler and rough shooter.

# GERMAN WIREHAIRED POINTER

Most of the early wirehaired pointers represented a combination of griffon, Stichelhaar (both mixtures of pointer, foxhound, pudelpointer and Polish water dog), pudelpointer (a cross of poodle and pointer) and German shorthair. The Germans had a preference for a hardier dog, and continued to breed the distinctive traits of pointer, foxhound and poodle until what is today's dog appeared. The longer coat is one of the distinctive features deliberately emphasized during breeding, lending an all-weather capability and protection against rough cover.

*German wirehaired pointer.*

## HUNGARIAN VIZSLA

One of the oldest of the HPR breeds, first recorded in 1350 but appearing in etchings dating from the tenth century, the Vizsla was selectively and exclusively bred by the Hungarian aristocracy. Medium-sized, with a short, russet-coloured coat, the Vizsla is highly intelligent and biddable, with a fast, wide-ranging hunting style; it hunts diligently at a pace that it can maintain all day, if necessary. As befits its breeding, it has an elegant, aristocratic air and attracts attention wherever it goes. In the home it is a gentle but excitable presence, very loyal – a Vizsla is always conscious of where its owner is, even when out in the field – and will always be all over you if you let it. Highly trainable, the Vizsla does not react well to harsh correction or voice – and they all have the ability to sulk for England.

*Hungarian Vizsla.*

*Hungarian wirehaired Vizsla.*

## HUNGARIAN WIREHAIRED VIZSLA

The wirehair is of Hungarian origin, created by crossing the short-coated Vizsla with a German pointer and later setter, with the intention of producing a more rugged and waterproof dog capable of work in rough terrain and water. The wirehair is a gentle dog with a sensitive nature, very biddable in training. It is very versatile in its work, both as a gundog and with falcons.

*Italian spinone.*

## ITALIAN SPINONE

This is a large, friendly dog with a relatively slow trotting gait, allowing it to hunt a large area methodically. The original representatives of the breed are not easy to trace, and opinions vary widely, but the coarsehaired setter and the white mastiff, prevalent along the coasts of the Italy, are the most likely candidates. The breed was introduced into the UK in 1981, gaining Kennel Club recognition in 1994.

## LARGE MUNSTERLANDER

The large Munsterlander originates in Germany and is essentially a German longhaired pointer. The GLP breed standard dictates that the colouring cannot contain black, and so the black and white Munsterlander could not be registered after 1908. In 1919 a group of enthusiasts met in Germany and decided to carry on with the black dog, and so founded the large Munsterlander.

*Large Munsterlander.*

## WEIMARANER

The distinctive silver-grey Weimaraner is a fairly recent development of the nineteenth century; it was used originally for big-game hunting in Germany on deer, wild boar, wolf and bear, for which it was used primarily as a tracking dog. Later on, when big game hunting was in decline, it was used increasingly on smaller game, such as rabbit, fox and increasingly game birds, its primary quarry today in the UK. It is not the best choice as a pet because it tends to attach itself to one person, which can be a source of conflict with others in the family.

*Weimaraner.*

# Chapter 3

# How to Choose your HPR

Most often it is the dog's outward appearance that is the major factor when a person decides which breed to choose: some may be captivated by the Brittany, others the aristocratic Vizsla or the ghostly Weimaraner. But could you live with them, and they with you?

## LONG HAIR VERSUS SHORT HAIR

Right from the outset, it is a good idea to consider whether a long-haired or short-haired dog would be best suited to your home. The long- or wire-haired varieties will shed hair naturally and will need to be groomed to keep the coat free from tangles, and to remove anything caught up in it – brambles, twigs, thorns and so on. The long hair will provide greater protection against injury and the elements, and so these varieties do not need to be docked: a working dog's tail is bound to incur damage, and the docking procedure is to spare a short-coated dog the pain of such injury. Their coats are waterproof, but will hold a surprising amount of water, as you will discover when they shake it off! Mud will need removing, most easily by letting it dry and then combing it out.

The short-haired dog will also shed hair, but usually in relatively small amounts, which is no problem for the vacuum cleaner; the coat is waterproofed with natural oils so water falls off with a brief shake, the dog being completely dry in a very short space of time. Mud is best left alone: it will dry quickly and will simply fall off; alternatively a very simple remedy is to get the dog to swim around for a minute so it washes out. Other, more unpleasant additions to the coat, such as fox droppings, along with the residue of gleeful rolling in other tempting mixtures, will need to be washed off under a hose or in a nearby stream otherwise they will linger on the coat and be unpleasant in the home. Short-haired dogs do groom themselves, and are generally quite clean.

The long-haired breeds are therefore higher maintenance, though not overly so; but you should consider the effect of a wet, muddy dog of either variety in your home.

## WHICH BREED?

Unless you already have a clear idea of the breed for you, some research is necessary. Game fairs, particularly the larger ones such as the CLA Game Fair and the Midland Game Fair, have a 'Discover Dogs' tent where most of the breeds can be found, and this provides the perfect opportunity to browse around and see them at first hand. Those manning the tents will be delighted to talk to you about their particular breed, and will answer you honestly, particularly in relation to the suitability of your home, the dog's reliability with children, its temperament and so on – so take your time to talk to those with the dog that pleases you most. Dog shows are another opportunity to view the various breeds and talk to the owners; these are to be found online at Fosse Data www.fossedata.co.uk and Higham Press www.highampress.co.uk. There are so many dog shows all over the country, there is bound to be one within easy reach for you to visit.

## SHOW DOG, WORKING DOG OR COMPANION?

It is important to decide whether your new dog will be a family companion, a pet, or if you would like to work it on a local shoot and possibly in field trials, because this will be the deciding factor in how you approach acquiring your new addition.

Let us be clear from the outset: a dog bred from an out-and-out working strain will be much more demanding to train, it will be more wilful, and it will become frustrated, and potentially very destructive and unhappy if its instincts and energies do not find their natural outlet. At the very least this will involve the owner in a lot of exercise and training. So if you are looking for a pet, do not get a working dog – it will almost certainly end in tears, with the risk of the dog having to be rehomed through the rescue services or a sanctuary.

The beginner wishing to acquire a dog to show would be advised to visit a few championship shows first: you will quickly come to see that many of the same faces, with their dogs, appear regularly, and are consistently placed in the final line-up to receive awards. Approach these exhibitors and talk to them about your plans – though don't try to strike up a conversation just before they are about to go into the ring! Bear in mind that the more successful the breeder is in the show ring, the more expensive the pups are likely to be.

While you are there, take time to soak up the atmosphere, see how the show works and watch how the top handlers show their dogs, from setting them up to running around the ring.

## YOU WANT A PET

HPRs do make wonderful pets, but not all are suited to family life: some breeds attach themselves to a single person and will not tolerate others, such as children or other dogs; others are perfectly content in the home environment. It is important to do your research, to talk to owners and breeders about your home situation, and to use the Internet to look up the breed club or society for the breed that interests you. There will be valuable information about the temperament to help you decide. You should also be aware that even though your pet may not come from working stock, this does not mean that it is any less in need of a lot of exercise: all the HPR breeds, pet or not, will require a substantial amount of daily exercise.

## DOG OR BITCH?

Another decision you will have to make is whether to have a dog or a bitch. In general terms, bitches will mature earlier than males – though don't assume that they will be any less energetic or less of a handful. They will also come into season (on 'heat') twice a year, although this cycle can be highly variable: some dogs have only one heat a year, or they cycle at different intervals, depending on the breed and the individual bitch (some bitches do have irregular seasons, or their first is very late). When they are on heat they will need to be isolated from other dogs – confined to the home premises, and not taken on walks where other dogs, particularly males, may be encountered for the twenty-one-day period that the cycle lasts. A bitch in season cannot compete, and will not be allowed on the grounds where a working test or field trial is taking place.

That all said, the situation is manageable if you know what the limitations are, and how they may be integrated and accommodated into your own particular home situation. Quite obviously, you will need a bitch if you are planning on breeding – the choice in the end is largely one of personal preference.

## THE BREEDER'S RESPONSIBILITY

The next step is to talk to some breeders. Most breeders feel a responsibility towards the development of their chosen breed, and to the welfare of the pups they produce. Unfortunately, there are also those who have no regard for the breed and are only interested in using it as a money-making machine for themselves, and who abuse the animals they keep: breeding from bitches that are too young, breeding too many litters from a single bitch, ignoring hip scores, and so on. It is a fact of life that where larger sums of money are concerned, the unsavoury and unscrupulous will be there. Ensure as well as you can that you acquire your dog from a responsible breeder.

A responsible breeder will have the welfare of the breed at heart, they will appreciate that its correct development is in their hands, and will take this responsibility very seriously. You can get a good feel for being on the right track by the questions they ask you. Sometimes it feels as if they don't actually want you to have a dog from them at all, but this is a good sign: they are merely making sure that yours will be a proper home, that you will be able to cope with the demands of the dog, and that it will fit into your lifestyle. Be encouraged by this, because it is a sure sign of a responsible breeder.

You must insist on seeing the hip scores and the pedigrees for both parents, and you should also insist that you visit the breeder at their home where you can see the pups with their mother. If they attempt to put you off or dodge the request, then do not deal with them any further. You can expect to be invited to see the litter after three weeks or so, and again later at around five weeks, to choose which pup you want, and a last visit to actually take your pup home.

### Docked or Undocked?

The breeder will make the choice as to whether any of the litter will be docked, and this will depend on whether the puppies are destined for homes requiring a dog for showing, or as a pet, or whether interest has been expressed for a working dog. Some breeders will not dock at all, while others who are breeding from working lines with the intention of finding working homes for the pups will have them all docked; others with enquiries for both working dogs and show dogs or pets may elect to have only a proportion of the litter docked.

### Choosing from the Litter

The breeder and the owner of the stud dog will have the pick of the litter if they wish, the rest being available to new prospective owners. So how do you choose? It is usually said that you should pick the most active or curious puppy, or the one that comes up to you immediately. This is a very unreliable method, however, as it does not take into account the fact that just as you arrive to pick out your pup, the ones that are usually the most active may have just fallen asleep – and pups do sleep a lot; and it is very difficult, if not impossible, to try and make a reasonable stab at identifying your perfect companion at such an early age, when you have only a short time to observe them. Of course the breeder will have been keeping a close watch on the whole of the litter, and may be able to point out individual characteristics; but again, this is no guide as to how they might develop as they get older. All in all, it is a lottery, and the choice will be largely down to the one that catches your eye. Once you have chosen your pup, stop worrying. The bonding process begin when you bring your puppy home.

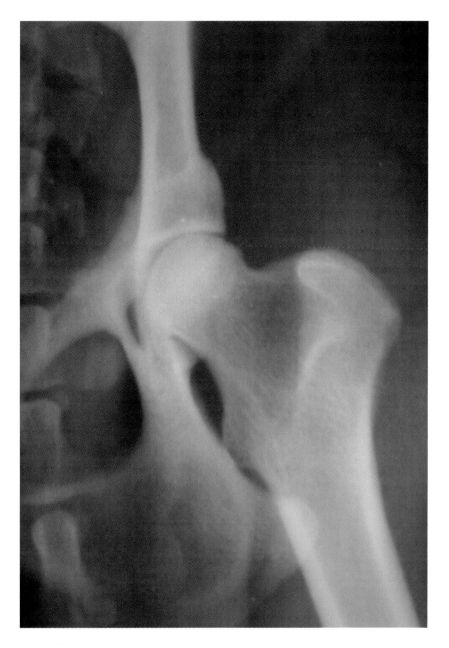

*Hip joint showing tight ball and socket structure.*

### Documentation

When the day comes for you to pick up your pup it is a good idea if two of you go so that it is not left on its own on what will most probably be the first time in the car. It will need reassurance – and not only this, but you are separating it from its mother, which is highly stressful and it is bound to cause a commotion during the journey.

The breeder should give you a puppy pack, often from one of the dog food manufacturers; this will contain information on how to introduce your new dog into its new home, the pedigree certificate (a five generation one is usual), and the Kennel Club registration certificate that you must use in order to change the ownership of the dog from the breeder's to your own.

## HIP SCORES

The HPR breeds are susceptible to hip dysplasia, a condition embracing certain defects in the structure of the hip, which are inherited from the parents. Essentially the socket and ball constituting the hip joint are imperfect in some way, and this can lead to lameness, with continuous pain. It is important to familiarize yourself with this condition because it affects all HPRs, and also to appreciate the importance of hip scoring, which is designed to reduce the condition and minimize its effects.

The following article is reproduced by kind permission of Verity J. Griffiths BSc(Hons), MA, VetMB, GPCert(SAS), MRCVS; it was first published in the Hungarian Vizsla Society newsletter in 2006, written with the Vizsla in mind, but it applies to all HPR breeds. You should check on the hip score recommendation for your breed – your vet will be able to advise, or you should contact the breed society.

### Hip Scores: What Does It All Mean?

Hip dysplasia is characterized by instability of the hip joint, and is a common and often debilitating orthopaedic condition affecting many of the larger breed dogs. It is generally considered that puppies are born with normal conformation of the hip joint – that is, a smoothly fitting ball-and-socket joint comprising the femoral head (the ball) and the acetabulum (the socket) (*see* opposite).

The mechanism by which dysplastic hips become lax and unstable is due to many factors, both genetic and environmental. In severe cases, this laxity of the soft tissues (muscles and ligaments supporting the hip joint) can be detected by your vet at first vaccination. Because it occurs in young dogs when the bones are still partly cartilaginous, these 'soft' joints, instead of ossifying into a normal, hard, bony, well fitting ball-and-socket conformation, develop to form a shallow, less congruous joint. Arthritic

new bone then forms due to stresses on the soft tissue components of the joint, and further remodelling changes occur (*see* page 26). The degenerative process then becomes a vicious cycle, one that is exacerbated by obesity and over-exercise.

In 1984 the British Veterinary Association (BVA), in association with the Kennel Club, instituted the BVA/KC hip dysplasia scoring scheme to replace the earlier pass/breeder's letter/fail scheme. Many countries have their own scoring system, but in the UK, a single radiographic ventro-dorsal pelvic view is used. The best X-rays are achieved with a relaxed dog using either sedation or general anaesthesia. The skeletally mature dog, over twelve months old, is usually laid in a trough on his/her back and the hind limbs are extended with the stifles parallel to each other – this is achieved by the strategic use of sellotape and ties! It is essential to have a marker to mark left or right, together with the date, and the dog's Kennel Club registration number, which will show on the film. This can be fiddly, because there are strict rules governing the suitability of an X-ray: there must be no rotation of the pelvis, and this can be difficult sometimes in very thin, bony dogs.

A diagnostic X-ray (*see* page 27) can then be submitted to the BVA together with the scoring fee and a part-completed certificate. The vet then signs to certify that the radiograph was taken on the date indicated, and may check and add the dog's microchip or tattoo number. Until the latter becomes mandatory, the substitution of dogs with known good hips could occur by unscrupulous breeders. One could consider this may be a case for DNA profiling to become more the norm.

The radiograph is then examined by two scrutineers, randomly paired, from a panel of (currently) thirteen, all who have been trained in hip dysplasia assessment. Annually these scrutineers have to undergo a quality control exercise to check their scoring is comparable, and as standardized as possible. Under the scoring

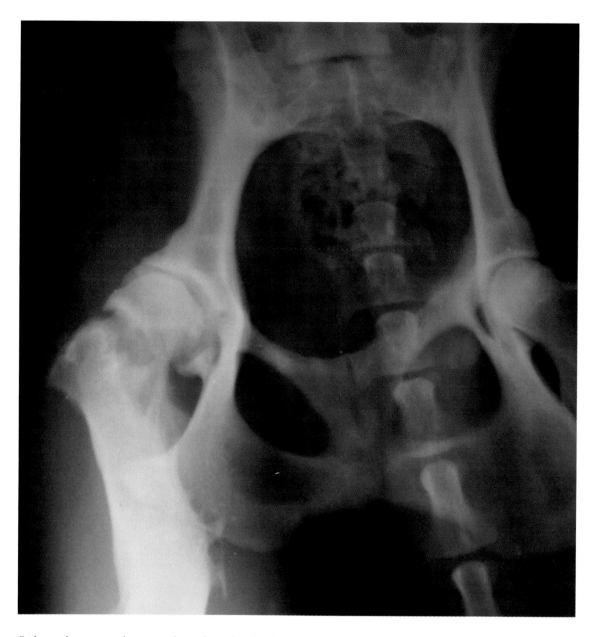

*End stage hip joint with severe arthritis due to hip dysplasia.*

scheme, nine radiographic features for each hip are assessed, with a numerical score given to each (0–6). Points are given to each undesirable feature, with zero being a perfect example of that feature. The individual scores are then added together to give a total for each hip, and hence a total score for the dog. Each feature is scored from 0–6, with the exception of one, the caudal acetabular edge, which is scored between 0–5. Thus the total parameters for each hip can range from 0–53 for a given dog, giving a possible total score of between 0 and 106 (*see* Table 1, page 28). This means that meaningful comparisons between dogs may be achieved.

As with most things, this system has its limitations and is by no means foolproof:

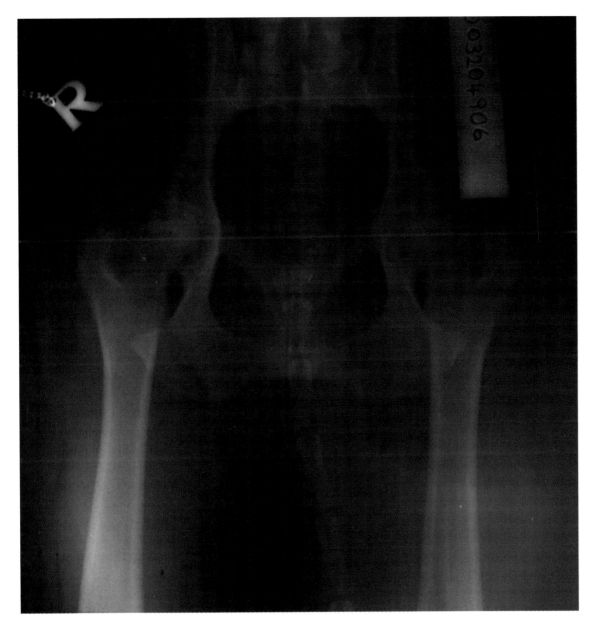

*Radiograph suitable for hip scoring (these scored 4/3; total 7).*

- It can only detect if a dog has reasonable hips, not whether the dog carries hip dysplasia genes.
- It cannot take into account environmental factors such as diet and bodyweight.
- The score does not take into account the age of the dog, except that it has to be over twelve months old.

- This a subjective scoring scheme and scrutineers do differ in opinion, hence the need for annual quality control to limit personal variations, and to ensure as far as is possible that scores do not have a large variance.
- Due to the complexities of genetics, relying on just a sire and dam with a low score may produce offspring with varying degrees of

| Hip Joint Radiographic Features | Score Range | Right | Left |
|---|---|---|---|
| Norberg Angle | 0–6 | *0* | *0* |
| Subluxation | 0–6 | *2* | *1* |
| Cranial acetabular edge | 0–6 | *2* | *2* |
| Dorsal acetabular edge | 0–6 | *0* | *0* |
| Cranial effective acetabular ridge | 0–6 | *0* | *0* |
| Acetabular fossa | 0–6 | *0* | *0* |
| Caudal acetabular edge | 0–5 | *0* | *0* |
| Femoral head/neck exostosis | 0–6 | *0* | *0* |
| Femoral head recontouring | 0–6 | *0* | *0* |
| **TOTALS 4/3 = 7 hip score** | | *4 (0–53)* | *3 (0–53)* |

*Table 1: Nine different parameters are measured; the scores are then summated to get a total hip score for the particular dog. In the case of the Labrador's x-ray shown on page 27, the results are shown in italic.*

hip dysplasia, which can obviously be very disappointing.

- Unfortunately there are some veterinary surgeons in practice who do little to support the scheme, and who bias the results by discouraging owners from submitting radiographs which they think may score highly.

As a summary of the scoring system, the lower the score the better, hip scores of 0,0 (total = 0) being perfect, and 53,53 (total = maximum 106) devastatingly dreadful. For each breed there is an average score obtained, which is continually being updated: this is known as the 'breed mean score' (BMS). The BMS for the Hungarian Vizsla is at present a total of twelve.

As breeders and as potential puppy purchasers, how is the scheme best used?

- Only breed from dogs with considerably less than the breed mean score (BMS). Currently for Hungarian Vizslas the BMS is twelve (up to 10/01/2005 after 930 hip scores were submitted). I personally would suggest that parents with scores of ten or less are chosen.

For example, a dog with 0,0 is excellent, 3,3 very good, 6,6 not so good but still within the breed average, whilst anything above this is not good so try to avoid it.

- Even if a mating is between two low-scored dogs, the offspring may still have varying degrees of hip dysplasia.
- The most helpful way of using the scoring information is in progeny testing, for example, selecting parents who are known to have previously produced offspring with good hips, as well as having good scores themselves.
- It has been proven that some dogs with good hips will consistently produce progeny with hip dysplasia, whilst others do not.
- Ideally it is important to research the hip scores of as many offspring of individual dogs before considering a match for breeding. Obviously, this can be more easily applied to sires as they are likely to produce more offspring in their lifetime.
- It's all in the genes! It is useful to check the grandparents, too, as their scores will have a bearing on the offspring.

- So by checking back through the line you can minimize the chances of throwing a pup with bad hips. But if in doubt as to the suitability of your dog to breed, it is best to seek advice from a vet who will have been sent the current breed mean scores when the certificate was returned to him/her, or ideally a vet who has an interest in orthopaedics.

Temperament and ability obviously all count in choosing the right match, but remember, it is theoretically possible for people who purchase a pup which develops hip dysplasia to sue a breeder who bred from affected parents.

In practice, the number of clients who continue to breed from their dogs either without hip scoring, or who, worse, ignore the score indication, is remarkably high, and this I find appalling. Likewise there are new puppy owners who look blankly at me when I ask what the parents' hip scores were; or they answer, 'Oh yes, the parents were hips scored,' but they have no idea what it means – and when investigated, it is revealed that the parents were indeed scored, but they had high scores and were therefore not suitable for breeding. All too often I have had to euthanase an otherwise healthy puppy because it can't bear its own weight, or it is suffering constant pain from severe hip dysplasia (*see* the image on page 31). I would prefer never to be put in this situation again, so I strongly urge responsible breeding in any breed, let alone that of my own preference, the Hungarian Vizsla.

Furthermore I strongly recommend that breeders advise prospective owners to insure their animals, because should the dysplasia problem arise, vets can do so much more when there are no financial constraints. In addition, I recommend the use of nutriceuticals – for example, glucosamine and chondroitin sulphate – during the skeletal development stage. These can be bought from agricultural suppliers and administered in feed, or ideally you could go for one of the extremely pure formulations presently available through your veterinary surgery, but on prescription only. There are others on the market, but I tend to subscribe to the thought that quality and purity come at a cost.

## Where Do I Get My Dog Hip-Scored?

Your vet is the first port of call. Specialist orthopaedic vets would be contactable by referral from your own vet, but often a practice has a vet with a keen interest in orthopaedics and with further training in the subject, who would be happy to assist.

## What Does It Cost?

British Veterinary Association rates for hip scoring as of 1 January 2008:

| Number of dogs scoring/ grading per dog | VAT inclusive charge |
|---|---|
| One to four | £35.40 |
| Five or more for the same owner | £28.20 |
| Rescoring under appeals procedure | £70.60 |
| Joint hip and elbow dysplasia submission | £63.30 |

In addition, there is a charge made by your vet to include sedation/general anaesthetic and X-ray; this cost varies from practice to practice. The author's practice, for example, currently charges an inclusive fee of £100 (including VAT).

## Anaesthetics

The anaesthetic issue is a hangover from the 'Good old days/James Herriot era'. Modern anaesthetics are extremely safe, the gold standard used by most practices being propofol induction and isoflourane (or cevoflourane) gaseous maintenance – these have come from the medical field where they are routinely used for ninety-year-olds having hip replacements! As long as a dog is fit and healthy there is minimal risk with any anaesthetic procedure.

The author's practice routinely uses a reversible sedation for hip scoring, which takes seven minutes to standing after reversing. This combination is medetomidine and butorphanol to sedate, and atipamizole to reverse the sedation. Again, this anaesthesia is extremely safe in young, fit animals – that is, the healthy breeding animal!

The risks of anaesthesia are infinitely preferable to the risks of producing crippled animals that will suffer, and will no doubt need long periods under anaesthetic to improve their quality of life.

The fear of the risks involved in the anaesthetic procedure should not be an excuse to avoid hip-scoring your dog.

## OTHER CONDITIONS

Other conditions that may affect your chosen breed include entropion, ectropion, dysphagia, hypothyroidism and idiopathic epilepsy: these are some that affect HPRs, as well as other breeds, and all of these possibilities should be carefully researched when you are looking to acquire your first dog. Some conditions may be more prevalent in one breed than another, in particular hereditary diseases (caused in the main by breeding from a small gene pool).

## CODE OF ETHICS/CODE OF CONDUCT FOR BREEDERS

Prior to mid-2008 most breed societies published codes of conduct for breeders. These set out the best practice for breeding: the minimum age for the bitch, the maximum age, the minimum time between litters, the availability of hip scores for both parents, and many other vital criteria.

From mid-2008 the Kennel Club has required breed societies to adopt its own code of ethics. Many societies feel that the Kennel Club code of ethics is not as stringent as their own breeds' codes of conduct and that valuable protection for their breed has been lost. Societies wishing to amend the Kennel Club code of ethics template with additional criteria must now apply to the Kennel Club for approval, or rejection, of their breed specific criteria. Check the code of ethics for your chosen breed society carefully, as it is likely to change as variations are approved by the Kennel Club.

## DOG RESCUE

There are many reasons why a dog is no longer wanted in the home: a change of circumstances such as divorce, change of job, moving to a smaller home, children, not coping with the demands of the dog or being unable to give it the attention it needs, along with a myriad of other situations, any of which may lead the family to the conclusion that the dog has to go. Too often, though, it is because the family has made the wrong decision in choosing an HPR dog.

The first port of call is always to the breeder from whom the dog was acquired, and the majority of breeders will want you to contact them if you have a problem. It is often difficult for the owner to admit that they don't want the dog any more, having gone through the rigmarole of convincing the breeder that the puppy is coming to a stable, loving home; now that their circumstances have changed, they are embarrassed to pick up the phone and confess to their predicament. Don't hesitate, however – call the breeder and explain. A responsible breeder will always take one of their dogs back for rehoming – but if this avenue fails, for

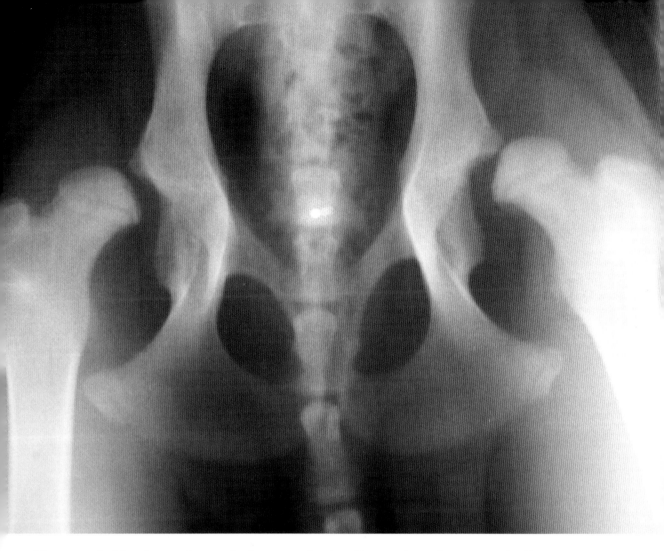

*This pup was bred from hip-scored parents for the purpose of working. He was euthanased at seven months old.*

whatever reason, the breed society for the dog in question will have a rescue programme.

It is preferable to use the specialized knowledge and contacts of the breed societies, rather than a dog sanctuary: the breed rescue is dedicated to the welfare of that particular breed, and will make extraordinary efforts to protect the dog and to find a suitable new home. It is also best placed to do so: with years of experience with a specific breed, the rescue workers are in the best position to judge whether a re-homing is likely to be successful.

# Chapter 4

# Showing the HPR

Most of us have seen Crufts on the television, even if we are not acquainted with the rest of the dog show world, but you will quickly find that it is very big business indeed. And while Crufts is the epitome of all the shows and the largest dog show in the world, there are many others to go to around the country.

For many, the dog show is a fun event where they can see lots of beautiful animals and have a good day out wandering round the rings and browsing in the many trade stands present at the larger shows. For the breeder, however, the show has a different meaning: here, the results of their breeding programme are scrutinized by

*Hands-on assessment: the judge must be able to assess the underlying structure of the dog.*

their peers, with success in the ring confirming the correctness of their line and being the stamp of approval that they are doing the right thing. Those engaged in serious breeding – that is, for the good of the breed, and not just as a money-making opportunity (which is the most reprehensible motive) – take great care with regard to the development of their stock, and strive to ensure that the best characteristics are maintained through successive generations while trying to ensure that any genetic faults are minimized, if not eliminated.

The HPR breeds are very popular at shows: the number of exhibits increases year on year, with organizers having to accommodate ever-larger class sizes. As a working gundog breed, the HPR is classed as a dual-purpose dog in that it is both worked on the shooting field and shown in the ring. In an ideal world, all the dogs shown would be working dogs, as was in fact the case when Crufts first came into being, and which is why it takes place in March – a short time after the end of the shooting season; today, however, the number of dogs that do both is relatively small, and the great majority of those appearing in the show ring have little or nothing to do with shooting, and will never be used as working gundogs.

## TYPES OF SHOW

Shows are not all about breeders, however, and the majority of those who exhibit their dog do it for the sheer fun and challenge. Maybe they start at a local event, or attend ringcraft classes regularly, as much as a social occasion as anything else; they may experience the excitement of winning, and moving up a level to exhibit at championship shows – and maybe, just maybe, the thrill of gaining a challenge certificate with show champion title is now a realistic goal. Showing your dog can be a fascinating hobby in its own right.

---

### A Word on Docking

Tail docking is not illegal. The Animal Welfare Act 2006 prohibits the showing of docked animals where the public pays to enter, but does not prohibit the traditional docking of certain *bona fide* working dogs. As the vast majority of those bred will not be worked, they will no longer be able to be docked legally, with the inevitable consequence that the undocked, long-tailed version of the breed will be the norm in the show ring. As docking is done to prevent damage to the dog's tail when it is working in the field, it follows that dogs that remain undocked will be at greater health risk if they are worked; those who work their dogs will continue to dock in the interests of the health of their dog, but by doing so will be barred from the show ring – except, of course, at those shows where the public does not pay to enter.

Vets can dock pups before they are five days old, but will require documentation to support the claim that they will be used for working. The production of a shotgun certificate by the owner of the stud dog, or a letter from a gamekeeper, will usually be sufficient.

---

### *Single Breed Shows*

As the name suggests, single breed shows are for a particular breed, organized by a breed club or society. Judges at these shows are usually breed specialists, with many years' experience of showing and breeding these dogs; and there will certainly be other breed specialists present, giving you the chance to talk to and learn from experts.

### *Companion Dog Shows*

The companion dog show is a relaxed event, held purely for fun and often associated with a fund-raising event. Such a show is not held under Kennel Club rules, which means that the show is free to exhibit any dog. There may be breed classes, gundogs for example, as well as 'Dog which looks most like its owner' or 'Dog with the biggest grin' to emphasize the fun element. Quite often you will find these shows at local fêtes, or as part of larger shows at your local showground. Many of the dog owners who have entered these shows have been inspired with enthusiasm, and this has led them to the show world, and the beginning of a new hobby.

## Open Shows

Open shows are held by dog clubs and the breed clubs or societies. As there are far more dog clubs than breed clubs, a great many open shows are held throughout the year. They are regarded as the training ground on the way to competing in the championship shows, and are run in exactly the same way as a championship show, under Kennel Club rules and with KC-approved judges.

## Championship Shows

The championship show (of which Crufts is one) is where a dog can be awarded a challenge certificate (CC or 'ticket'). The CC is the highest award available, and winning three CCs under three different judges will qualify your dog as a show champion and allow you to use the sought-after 'Sh. Ch' prefix (gundogs use the 'Show Champion' – 'Sh. Ch' – prefix unless they have gained a field trial award, or SGWC, which confers full 'champion' status). Championship shows are run by dog clubs and breed societies under Kennel Club rules; they are also the place to qualify your dog for Crufts. The championship show is a 'benched' show: a 'bench' is really a small, three-sided pen located close to the ring where you will be showing, and where your dog must be exhibited when it is not in the ring. On acceptance of your entry you will be allocated a number, and this will correspond to the bench place where your dog will be exhibited during the show.

## Show Gundog Working Certificate (SGWC)

To achieve full champion status, a gundog needs to have a recognized working qualification to provide proof of its natural working ability – these qualifications are gained in the field at field trials and include any award, including a Certificate of Merit (COM) or the Show Gundog Working Certificate. The requirements to pass a SGWC are less rigorous than those required to gain a field trial award, but the dog must still show natural working ability, and be able to retrieve game to hand; absolute steadiness to flush and shot is not required. The SGWC may be gained at a field trial or at a show gundog working day.

To enter a field trial as a SGWC competitor you will need to contact the field trial secretary of the society running the trial concerned, and ask if they will accept a SGWC entry; if so, you will need to obtain an entry form to enter the field trial, as any other competitor. An entry of over twelve dogs will trigger a ballot, from which the final twelve will be decided. The field trial secretary will convey the result of the draw to all entrants.

If you are lucky enough to get a 'run', the field trial secretary will already have had the agreement of the judges to an SGWC entry, but when you are called into line you will need to tell them so they know how to assess your performance correctly. It is worth noting that although the standard of the dog's performance to achieve an SGWC is less than that required to achieve a field trial award, if your dog performs with sufficient merit it can earn a field trial award proper.

## Finding a Show

The easiest way to find a show is to search online. Most are listed on either the Fosse Data or Higham Press websites but you may well find smaller, local shows in the local press. Many of the larger show events held on your local showground often hold smaller dog shows, and you will often find show schedules laid out at your ringcraft club.

## Getting Started

The best and easiest way to get started is to join the local ringcraft club. These classes are usually held in the local village hall, so a good place to start is to enquire there, as well as asking your local vet. Ringcraft classes teach you how to 'stand' your dog – how to best present it to the judges – and how to run it round the ring so its natural movement is shown to best advantage. It takes time and effort to learn how to present a dog at a show: you and your dog must make a happy team, and exhibiting correctly is not as easy as it may first appear. Ringcraft will teach you how to present your dog so that its finer points are brought out, and how its not-so-fine points can be, if not disguised, at least turned to better advantage.

The classes are very sociable events for both you and the dog, and it certainly pays to socialize your dog as early as possible so that it becomes accustomed to being around many dogs, and to the strange sounds that it will find at the bigger shows. Many ringcraft clubs run companion dog shows or matches for members to gauge how they are progressing. Before going to ringcraft, your dog must already have had some basic obedience training (sit, stay, heel): this you can gain at local obedience or training classes, which again you can find out about by asking your local vet.

## JUDGING

### The Breed Standard

The starting point for all show judges is the breed standard. All Kennel Club-recognized breeds have a breed standard, which is a detailed description of the ideal dog: you can find the standard for your dog either at the Kennel Club website or with one of the breed clubs or societies. Since the ideal dog is rarely, if ever, encountered, the job of the judge in the show ring is to decide which of the dogs being shown is the closest match to the breed standard, and more subjectively, which pleases their eye. However, while the breed standard can define

the ideal attributes, it cannot define movement, attitude, or even the 'star quality' that sets the top show dog above the rest.

All judges are highly experienced at their craft, and will have judged many hundreds of dogs over a number of years before they are considered qualified to award challenge certificates at the championship shows. At single breed shows the judge is usually a breed specialist, with an intimate knowledge and experience of the chosen breed.

### Standing Your Dog

Standing the dog at the start and the end of a class gives judges the opportunity to assess each dog in terms of its conformation in accordance with the breed standard, and enables them to pick out for closer examination those that immediately catch the eye. Ringcraft will have taught you how to stand your dog correctly, placing its feet correctly at the front and back so it is not overstretched, with the head held properly, and the tail held to ensure a clean line along the length of the dog.

### Hands-On Assessment

When it is your turn, the judge will approach you for the hands-on assessment, starting with the eyes, the appearance and shape of the head, and noting the set and length of the ears. The mouth will be gently opened to allow the teeth and bite to be checked. With a hand on each side, the neck will be felt to assess the muscling. The forequarters and the shoulders will be checked, also the elbows, which should be straight and not pointing in or out.

The feet are assessed as to whether they are tight or not, also the set of the legs, whether they are too far apart or too close together, and whether the feet point forwards or are pointing out or inwards. The judge will run their hands along the body to check the muscling, they will assess by eye the length of the back, the height

of the withers, and the broadness of the chest, and its depth. The tightness of the belly and the ribs are noted. The hindquarters are assessed for muscling and for straightness, also to check that there is no cow hock, and that the dog has the correct angulation.

Moving away from the dog, the judge will again assess the visual purity, the topline in particular and the angulation, front and back.

### Round the Ring

Running the dog round the ring allows the judge to assess its gait and movement: it is important here to run the dog at the speed at which its movement is best presented – a fast trot, not breaking into a run, is usually best. Judges will usually ask you to run the dog once round the ring and then along the diagonal directly away from them, turning to come back towards them. As you run round the ring they will be assessing movement, power and drive, the firmness of the dog's back, whether it is roached or straight, and the overall visual impact of the topline. The side view allows assessment of the angle of the croup and rear angulation, which, when correct, should result in the proper breed-typical movement.

As the dog is going away from the judge they will be assessing the hocks and the movement of the rear, overall balance, and the set of the feet and tracking. Moving towards the judge allows them to assess the whole of the front, whether the feet are in line with the shoulders, and the straightness, or not, of the elbows. Apart from these technical aspects, judges will be assessing the overall temperament of the dog, whether it is happy or not, and will notice the character that springs from the dog: the winning dog enjoys what it is doing, and has that indefinable 'ring presence' that lights up the ring, setting the show champion above the rest.

*OPPOSITE: The final line-up, waiting for the judges' decision.*

*Impress the judge with your dog's movement and gait*

Having completed their assessment, the judge will ask you to run round the outside of the ring to join the back of the waiting line. This gives another assessment opportunity – although usually the judge has already turned to view the next exhibit.

### The Final Line-Up

The judge will have been making mental notes as to the exhibits that have been the most pleasing, and the final line-up gives them the opportunity to view again those that are uppermost in their mind, and to sort them into the final placings. With a large class, the judge may discard the lesser exhibits so that the contenders coming into the final line-up are brought down to a more manageable number. Decision made, the winning dogs are indicated by the judge, and are brought forwards. The first-placed dog is the first to be brought to the winners' line-up, where they will receive their awards, rosettes and any other prizes on offer. Judges must provide a written assessment of the top-placed dogs, and may request that they are lined up so their final impressions, and the dog's finer points, may be recorded.

If you were not chosen as one of the winners, don't be discouraged, but remember that judging is essentially subjective, and what may please one judge may not impress another at a different show. Keep in mind that it can take a while for all the pieces to fall into place for you, and that there is a learning curve for you to climb. Roll on the next show!

## AGILITY SHOWS

Fast and furious, highly entertaining and addictive, dog agility is a popular spectator sport and great fun for both the competitor and their dog. Introduced in 1978 at Crufts by the Kennel Club, the agility competition was originally designed to be a spectacle to liven up the show day: well, it certainly does that, with the crowds appreciating and cheering on the dogs as they jump over hurdles, weave through the poles and balance along a see-saw, racing round the course against the clock. Agility has grown steadily in popularity, with all types of breeds now active in the sport – including HPRs. The HPR is a highly intelligent animal that requires mental as well as physical stimulation – both of which are provided in abundance by participation in, and training for, agility competitions.

It is a type of competition in which the fitness and agility of dog and handler team is tested round a course of obstacles. There are well over 300 agility events licensed by the Kennel Club around the country, as well as training clubs and informal agility competitions at fêtes and country shows. There are four types of agility event:

*Agility is popular with the crowd, and the dog. (Photo courtesy of Nick Ridley)*

---

### Agility Show Obstacles

**'A' ramp** An 'A'-shaped ramp formed by two ramps with a non-slip surface and anti-slip slats: dogs must climb over it.

**Brush fence** This is another sort of hurdle, again with an easily displaced top unit.

**Collapsible tunnel** A rigid, round entrance with the body of the tunnel made of non-slip cloth up to 3m (10ft) long.

**Cross-over** A raised, square table with ramps leading up to all four sides. The dog must go up and down the particular ramps indicated by the judge.

**Dog walk** A plank approximately 1.3m (4ft 6in) high, with firmly fixed ramps at each end.

**Hoop (tyre)** A hoop or tyre suspended from a frame at a fixed height.

**Hurdles** A maximum of 65cm (25in) in height and 1.2m (4ft) in width.

**Long jump** The dog must jump a maximum length of 1.5m (4ft 11in), clearing a series of low jumps.

**Pause box** An area 1.2m by 1.2m (4ft by 4ft) on the ground of the ring, where the dog has to pause for a period specified by the judge.

**Pipe tunnel** A minimum of 60cm (2ft) wide and up to 3m (10ft) long.

**Rising spread jump** Two hurdles positioned closely together with the first hurdle set lower than the second.

**See-saw** A plank at least 3.6m (12ft) long, mounted on a pivot or fulcrum.

**Table** The table is a minimum of 90cm (3ft) square, and the dog must lie down on it for a time set by the judge.

**Water jump** A low hurdle in front of a jump of shallow water.

**Weaving poles** A row of five to twelve poles set at least 45cm (18in) apart. The dog has to weave its way through them without missing one.

**Wishing well, or lych gate** A type of jump that has a roof on it.

---

| | |
|---|---|
| Agility matches: | Limited to members of the promoting society |
| Limited agility matches: | Limited to members, certain breeds or sizes |
| Open agility: | Open to all |
| Championship: | At which agility certificates can be won |

Size does matter in agility, and each dog must fit into one of the categories of small, medium or large. The size of the dog is determined by measuring its height at or under the withers: thus small dogs can be up to 35cm (13¾ in), medium dogs must be over 35cm but not exceed 43cm (17in), and large dogs over 43cm (17in). Every dog entered for competition must first be measured by an approved Kennel Club measurer, who will give out a certificate indicating for which size class the dog is eligible.

Agility competitions have many different classes, becoming progressively more difficult: thus you move through the ranks of Elementary, Starters, Novice, Intermediate, Seniors, Advanced and Open. The competition ring will consist of sixteen obstacles, the dimensions of which vary according to the dog size.

Each show has a new course designed for it, and the judge for the day will calculate the time for the course to be run, based on its length; dogs will be expected to complete the course within this time limit, and 'time faults' will be added if a dog exceeds it – one fault for each second over the set time. The run is usually timed manually, but in championship classes electronic timing equipment must be used. Faults are added to the dog's actual time if it fails to negotiate an obstacle, or if it negotiates it incorrectly. The dog with the fastest time and the least number of faults – that is, with a clear round – will be the winner. The list of faults that incur penalties, and the faults that result in the dog being immediately eliminated from the competition, is quite long and complex; however, it is set out in detail in the KC (H) regulations, a copy of which can be obtained from the Kennel Club at a nominal charge. Anyone competing in agility classes should be acquainted with the regulations, so it's a good idea to arm yourself with a copy of them.

An agility course arena is about 35 x 35yd (32 x 32m) in size, so it isn't something that everyone can have in their back garden; however, there

*A Weimaraner negotiates the tunnel. (Photo courtesy of Nick Ridley)*

are many clubs spread around the UK which have the facilities. You can locate your local agility club by consulting the websites listed at the end of this chapter. The pinnacle of achievement in agility is the award of 'Agility Champion' and the right to use the 'Ag. Ch.' suffix, awarded to those dogs that have received three agility certificates under three different judges.

Sixteen obstacles to be negotiated means sixteen situations for the dog to be trained to master and practise, so that each is completed as quickly as possible. Each obstacle is a little challenge in its own right, and it will take commitment from both the dog and owner to work on them consistently at agility club level. Luckily most dogs really enjoy this kind of work, and the majority of the HPR breeds are well suited to this disciple – except probably the Italian Spinone, which with its typical slow trotting style is wholly unsuited to what is essentially about beating the clock. However, all the other breeds are eminently suited to this sort of competition, and many appear in the agility league tables.

# Chapter 5

# The HPR as a Shooting Dog

We have seen how the various breeds have been selectively bred over the years to work in the field with a hunter to help him find game to put on the dinner table. Today there are many more HPR dogs to be found in homes as pets, and these will never be expected to work in their original capacity as a hunter, and their owners probably have no idea of the hunter role their dog was bred for. Many breeders are concerned with success in the show ring rather than in the field, their breeding programmes guided by the dog's look and structure rather than its ability as a gundog, and ultimately this will result in animals whose hunting instincts become

*Guns wait for the retrieve.*

*German wirehaired pointer quartering for game.*

progressively diminished and finally extinguished altogether. And while it is true that the pet may be perfectly happy as a family companion, it does seem a waste of all the natural ability and intelligence inherent in these unique breeds.

Happily, many people do use the HPR as a shooting dog, although while its popularity continues to grow, the HPR is still definitely in the minority on the average shoot, which is dominated by labradors and spaniels. And for good reason: as the driven shoot came to the fore, with the beating line working up towards a line of guns waiting on their pegs, the need was for dogs to work just in front of the advancing line, pushing the birds ever forwards or flushing them out if they are sitting tight, hidden in the middle of brashings or bracken unnoticed by the beater. This continuous advance is designed to encourage the maximum number of birds to fly forwards and over the waiting line of guns. And when the drive is over, the dogs must find and retrieve all the fallen birds not already found and

retrieved by those guns with their own picking-up dog beside them on the peg.

This scenario is at odds with the way a hunt, point, retrieve dog works. While the spaniel busily quarters from side to side, it is rarely more than a few yards away from its handler; the HPR, in contrast, will hunt on its own ahead of between one to three or four guns, ranging wide on either side of the handler – up to 100 yards or so on either side is usual – and methodically covering large expanses of ground as it searches for game. As soon as it finds game, it will point, and will stay on point allowing the guns to arrange themselves around the dog ready to shoot when the bird is flushed into the air by the dog on command. If the bird is shot, the dog is sent to retrieve it. This is the nature of the rough or walked-up shoot, with the dog equally at home working in woodland, up and down hedgerows, or ranging wide on open ground, over sugar beet or fodder crops.

While the HPR is well adapted to this kind of working, it does not fit so well with the more popular modern driven shoot. The spaniel will flush any bird it encounters, while the HPR will point it – and will stay pointing until the handler gets up to it and commands it to flush; however, this is not what is required in the driven shoot, when time spent walking up to dogs on point would be considered time wasted. A more likely scenario is that the many spaniels working ahead would take no notice of the dog diligently pointing his bird, but would rush up and flush it in front of the poor HPR, who, after similar treatment over a number of drives, may simply give up pointing altogether.

The problem is, if you want to work your dog on the local shoot it is most likely to be a driven shoot, so it is important to be able to fit in and be useful: more on this later. But first, let us understand how the HPR works in the field.

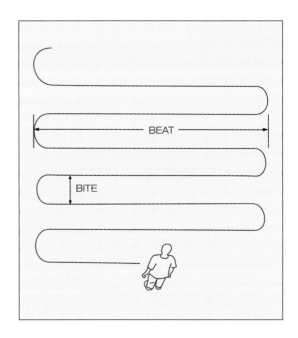

*The HPR's quartering pattern when questing for game.*

## HOW THE HPR HUNTS

To locate game, the dog uses its highly sensitive nose to pick up traces of the scent that is given off by game and carried on the wind. On an open field or in open woodland where there is sufficient room, to maximize its chance of catching a whiff of scent, the HPR will naturally run a wide pattern from side to side directly across the direction of the prevailing wind, turning upwind at the end of its beat to cross in front again, and so on up the field. This quartering pattern maximizes the chance of catching any scent. Most HPR dogs can maintain this running pattern for a long time, allowing one dog alone to cover a huge area of ground – it is a highly efficient game-finding strategy.

The width of the beat a dog runs is determined by the dog itself and by the nature of the terrain encountered. On the grouse moors, where game can be dispersed over a very large area, it is ideal for the dog to be able to range a long way out on either side of the handler. On a smaller local shoot the width of the beat will be determined by the width of the field, if

smaller, or more usually the distance between two guns placed out on either side of the handler. Remember that while a dog that runs out a quarter of a mile each side of its beat may look spectacular, there is the possibility that it will find and point game at the edge of the beat, which the guns then have to get to. In sugar beet or heather, this would be quite a slog. To keep the dog within the bounds of a reasonable length of beat, the handler uses the whistle to turn the dog if it is going out too far.

At the end of the beat, the dog will turn into the wind and start on its way back. The upwind distance between the line it is now running and its previous beat line is termed the bite. In good scenting conditions, a dog sensing that game may be around and ahead of it, will take a smaller bite to reduce the possibility that it is turning to run in front of game which it could not then scent. In doing so, it is making ground more slowly at the cost of using more of its energy, but it is doing so in the belief that it is highly likely to find its quarry, and so is worth the extra effort. Conversely, sensing the scenting conditions are not so good, it will take a larger bite to enable it to cover non-productive ground more quickly and so conserve its energy for the longer hunt.

Dogs will hunt at very different speeds depending upon the breed, its age, experience and the prevailing conditions; thus some run at full tilt all the time, while others have a more measured approach, matching their speed to suit the scent, which allows them to continue to hunt for a very long time.

The wind has a profound influence on how an HPR dog hunts, and the finer points of the effects of wind are covered in detail in Chapter 10, Field Trials.

*German shorthaired pointer on point.*

## GAME-FINDING

We know that an HPR is a fine companion to the rough shooter, with its senses tuned to locate game, with some better at it than others. A good game finder does not just denote the dog that is good at its task, namely a good hunter, good pointer and good retriever: it is all of those things, but with that extra common sense and instinct that enables it always to find something where others on the same ground cannot, even when there seems to be little game about. Some can show brilliant instinct by, for example, knowing that game is in the middle of a

hedge and running forwards: the dog runs along the outside until it is ahead, then turns and successfully holds and points its quarry, which has had to stop.

And how does it know when it's ahead of the quarry? Well, the scent is being carried to the dog on the wind, but as it moves level with the game the scent will become less apparent, and when it passes in front of the game all the scent will now be carried away from the dog, and it can work out that this is the time to stop, turn and point. You can't teach it. Dogs learn by experience how to handle and react to certain situations, but the good game finder seems to have it already built in and working.

## THE POINT

The most marvellous and arresting sight is that of a dog on a staunch point. This magical and totally instinctive action is one of the wonders of the gundog world. As the dog catches a strong enough scent it freezes in the direction of the scent, its body canted forwards, pointing directly at the game, tail held straight back and unmoving. This is a moment of truth for the game and the dog: the bird is now counting on its stillness to mask its presence, but the dog is there, fixed on the bird which cannot move, frozen by the deadly choice of moving and giving its position away, or the deadlock of sitting where it is and hoping.

A good dog on point will not move: its breeding and instinct locks it rigid in its position, and it will remain like this, if not for ever, at least for a very long time. This is called a staunch point. At other times the dog may not be totally sure there is something there, nose held higher, scenting the air, trying to work out what it is and where it is. Adopting more of a stalk now, moving carefully forwards, perhaps with one of its front paws held up in the air as it pauses to reassess. (This latter position is often used in photographs and is often seen in magazines, on websites, society logos and so on – but while it may be photogenic, it is actually the dog in a state of uncertainty.) When the dog is certain that game is there, and close enough, the whole body will stiffen, its feet on the ground and its body, tail and head immobile – a picture of intensity.

All working HPR owners have experienced their dog apparently 'lost', but eventually, having searched the wood where they were walking, whistling and shouting themselves hoarse, they finally come across the dog still diligently on point. From a practical point of view, this is good news. Say the dog is on point two hundred yards away. The handler, with gun, has to be able to make this distance in order to have a sporting chance of a shot. If the dog moves, the bird may flush, and the chance is gone. It is imperative that the dog 'holds' the bird until the handler can get up close to the dog to control the flush, and until the gun or guns arrive and have positioned themselves. Only then, and on command, should it 'get in' and flush the bird into the air.

Pointing is a totally instinctive thing. It cannot be trained, and a dog will either start to point on its own, or it won't. HPRs will point unless it has been bred out of them. This can happen when the breeding is for the show ring or to produce pets. With lack of practice the instinct will gradually diminish until it is no longer present – this can happen after about five generations. This is the same with any unpractised skill. Some dogs may start to point at a very young age, after four or five months, given the right environment with game around and therefore plenty of scent; whereas a dog kept in a largely urban setting and taken for its run in the local park will most likely not come across scent that its instincts would have urged it to point, and kept in this environment it will probably not be capable of pointing as it gets older.

Quite often a dog will go on point when you don't want it to. For example, walking along on the lead it suddenly goes on point into a neighbour's hedge. Dragging it away from a staunch

*Slovakian rough-haired pointer takes scent.*

point requires considerable effort, particularly if it is a large dog – and in any case is not the best thing to do: after all, you want to encourage your dog to do what it is doing, and yanking it off its point is sending a conflicting message to it, that this is not what you want it to do. The dog cannot be expected to know that it's quite all right to point a bird when it is off the lead in the shooting field, but it's not all right to point the same kind of bird in the neighbour's hedge. The thing to do in this situation is to reassure the dog, as before, and praise it as a 'Good boy' and stroke it for a while, but then gradually move it away, bodily if necessary, until it leaves the point. Walking two or three dogs that suddenly all go on point is more of a challenge, however!

The attitude of the dog on point can also tell us something about the prevailing scenting conditions: on point with its nose parallel to the ground the dog is pointing a bird some distance ahead of it, as the scent has travelled quite some distance – this is an indication of good scenting conditions. If the dog's body and nose are angled downwards, the bird will be very close to the end of its nose: this is an indication that the scent is not carrying very far, so the dog had to be very close before it caught the scent – therefore unfavourable scenting conditions.

'Flash pointing' describes the situation where a dog has just about passed a bird when it catches the scent, and its nose whips back round to point – but the bird immediately flushes without the dog having the chance to 'hold' it on its point. This is usually caused by a combination of unfavourable scenting conditions, and a back and/or cheek wind. It can also occur when the dog is just coming to the end of its beat and turns just fractionally short of a sitting bird which it is able, at the last moment, to scent, but it cannot stop to point it properly before it lifts.

With some dogs it is possible to tell the type of game being pointed: most commonly, when the dog is on point with one of its hind legs lifted slightly, this usually indicates that it is pointing a rabbit. Not all dogs do this, and it certainly cannot be trained, but a dog that does it anyway can be encouraged, so that on subsequent occasions its reflex becomes more pronounced and eventually it will always do it.

It has already been mentioned earlier that a dog on point with a front paw lifted is not sure of its ground, and is in a state of uncertainty. In this situation the thing to do is to encourage the dog to move closer and investigate ('What is it? What is it?') in the hope that it can sort out whether it is some residual scent, a rabbit moving about in cover, or if there really is a bird there, and by moving closer is able to point it, or nothing. But encourage the dog to do something – standing there looking good is fine for the photographer, but is otherwise unproductive and wasting time.

## ON SCENT

It is often quoted that the dog's nose is 10,000–1,000,000 times more sensitive than that of the human. This is an impressively big number, but it doesn't really help us to understand what it means to the dog.

It is difficult for us humans to really appreciate the paramount importance of the dog's nose, and it helps to understand their behaviour if we understand that the eyes are not the primary sensory tool for the dog as they are for us.

The dog will trust its nose first, and then use its other senses to back up what it is interpreting through it. This can quite readily be seen when there are game birds around in front of the dog, in plain sight of the owner, who wonders why the dog hasn't seen them running ahead – it is because the dog is using his primary sense organ – his nose – in overdrive mode to locate the source of the scent and home in on it. But don't, for one minute, mistake this for bad eyesight. A dog's eyesight is excellent, but is generally better at detecting movement; thus it can quite easily pick up the small movement of a rabbit, say, at hundreds of yards and without having yet caught its scent. If you now send the dog away, it will use the mark it made with its eyes and run towards that mark, and upon reaching it, use its nose to catch the scent trail to lead it to the quarry.

So what actually is scent? Every animal has its own peculiar scent, which is caused by tiny liquid particles excreted by the body and carried away by the wind. In humans, sweating is the primary means by which we lose liquid to the atmosphere (and by doing so the body is enabled to closely control its temperature), and will have a distinctive aroma. Furthermore, our bodily aroma changes with our state of mind – as we become excited or frightened, the production of adrenalin within the body will taint the sweat, which will now carry a different message to a dog: this is precisely how a dog can 'smell fear'.

Some animals have specialized glands that are designed to eject their aroma into the atmosphere and communicate meaning to other similar animals, such as the readiness to mate, or warning smells to potential predators. Of course, scent is not just given off by the human body: almost everything has its own trademark smell, some of which the human can sense, and some which it can't. Dogs can be trained to detect drugs hidden in suitcases, and to bark when they detect blood or explosives, making them a valuable asset to the security services. We, however, are concerned with the scent that the HPR is bred to detect: that of game.

Airborne scent is that which is carried on any prevailing wind and, however slight it may be, will carry the scent particles considerable distances. For the HPR, a light breeze carrying the scent downwind from the source is perfect. Strong, gusty winds will disrupt the passage of the scent, scattering it and perhaps trapping it in upward or sideways eddies so the dog has little chance of catching it – or if it does, it may not be able to follow it, as it is being constantly 'interrupted' as another gust carries the scent away. A light breeze over a constant, level landscape with little to disrupt the airflow is the perfect scenario for the hunting HPR, the dog quartering with a high head carriage in order to continuously air-scent the prevailing wind.

In still conditions, the probability of scent being carried is much lower, and the dog will adjust its head to scent closer to the ground in an effort to pick up foot scent: this is termed 'ground scenting'. Observing the head carriage of the dog provides the handler with good information as to the prevailing conditions.

Other local terrain characteristics, as well as the weather, all have their influence on scent. Very cold or very wet conditions are generally not conducive to good scent, while slightly warmer, drier conditions and a light breeze are better. Equally bad for scenting are hot, dry, windless days. A dip in the terrain may hold a pocket of scent, but a dip which is very cold may not. Walls and lines of trees disrupt the airflow upwards, often looping back and down and providing a confusing scent which the dog

*The HPR is bred to scent game.*

may find difficult to interpret; it is not unusual to see a dog staunchly pointing in a completely unexpected direction near to such obstacles.

Game that is standing or running will have a greater area of its body in contact with any airflow, so more scent will be carried away downwind; but when the bird is sitting on the ground with only the upper body in contact with the airflow, a much reduced quantity of scent can become airborne. Also, the parts of the bird in contact with the ground – its chest and underside – are the warmest, and it is these that would normally impart the most scent to the moving air. So by sitting, the bird is minimizing the amount of scent that is carried from it. Unfortunately for it, this is rarely a good defence against a capable HPR.

The scent from a live bird is very different to that of a dead one, and the HPR can tell the difference: it will point a live bird, but it won't point a dead one or one that is wounded or damaged (young, inexperienced dogs may do this, but they quickly learn the difference), and it knows it has to find the fallen bird or a 'runner' and retrieve it. A dead bird, however, will lose scent rapidly because the secretions have stopped, leaving only residual scent to be imparted to the air, and this will be exhausted after a period of time. How quickly this happens depends on the temperature of the bird in relation to the ambient outside temperature, and the strength of the wind: these are the biggest factors. Partridge, however, mask their scent immediately if they happen to fall breast down, and can be very difficult even for the most capable retriever to find.

Amazingly, the HPR can also tell the difference between scent emanating from a bird in front of it – which it points – and the scent left on the ground by a bird that has been sitting or standing for a while in one place but which has recently departed. For example, a bird sitting happily sunning itself decides that discretion is the better part of valour and runs off on

hearing a shooting party in the distance, leaving as it does a patch of scent on the ground where it was sitting and also a scent trail left by its feet. This residual scent will be picked up by the dog, which may slow down, and even stop to investigate, but will eventually acknowledge that the bird has departed, and will move on. Scent left by the feet may cause the dog to start tracking the scent trail, if it is recent enough for the dog to think it is worthwhile following, and it does so with its nose fractionally above the ground – moving sometimes alarmingly fast in a straight line down the field. Hare and rabbit are often the source of such ground-scenting trails.

## More About Scent

Scent is created by secretions from the skin and/or feathers or fur, which may be further tainted by chemicals in the animal that impart a certain smell or combination of odours – for example, adrenalin. These smells or odours are further modified by bacterial action on the surface of the skin, feather or fur. In humans, this has been often demonstrated by experiment, particularly by the manufacturers of deodorants: if a sterile sample of sweat is added to a culture, no detectable human odour will result even after many days; but adding bacteria to another sterile sample will produce odour within a short space of time. The liquid chemical complex from the animal is then imparted to the environment, primarily by evaporation, the speed or rate of which is influenced by a variety of environmental factors. We know that the rate of evaporation is influenced by temperature, surface area and volatility (which is closely coupled to the value of the latent heat of vaporization). Evaporation is a familiar phenomenon: we all know that water evaporates, and we all know that petrol evaporates faster, because it is more volatile – it has a lower boiling point, so requires less thermal energy

---

**Latent Heat**

Changes of state from liquid to vapour to gas require additional energy at each stage: this is termed latent heat, now called *enthalpy of vaporization*. 'Latent' means 'invisible', and refers to the pouring in of extra energy until there is enough stored up to trigger the change to the next state. If a thermometer is put into a kettle it will record the rise in temperature, as expected, as the water is heated. Nearing boiling point the rate of temperature rise slows and halts – so even though the kettle's heating element is still belting out the same amount of heat, it is no longer causing a rise in temperature. What is happening is that the energy is being absorbed into the water to enable it to turn, when it has absorbed enough, into steam (the 'change of state'), at which point the temperature again begins to rise rapidly.

---

(heat) to enable the change of state from liquid to vapour.

Are we then saying that scent is a liquid or a vapour? A vapour is a mixture of a substance in two states. In the case of water, vapour consists of water droplets in the liquid state and water in the gas state (steam). Scent then starts out as a liquid chemical complex, but warmed by body heat turns into a vapour, which is then carried away by moving currents of air. But remember that warm air is capable of absorbing more moisture into it than cold air, so the warm, moving air is able to take up the scented liquid on the body's surface as it evaporates. It may surprise you to learn that a veritable current of moving air exists around an animal's body, be it game bird or human being. Air close to the body is warmed by conduction, causing it to rise, which in turn creates a continuous convective upward movement of air from the body of the game – the perfect recipient and carrier for the odour vapours being generated close to the animal, and for the warm air to absorb liquid aroma, carrying both away as scent. Any prevailing wind will accelerate further dispersion throughout the environment.

The rate at which the scent is imparted is also to a large degree dependent upon the relative temperature of the environment and the body emitting the scent, with warm bodies in a cool environment giving off proportionally more scent than warm ones in a hot environment – meaning that the differential temperature gradient is important. Conversely, the rate of loss of thermal energy – cooling – of any body is proportional to the excess temperature (Newton's law of cooling): this means that the temperature of a body will fall faster to begin with, but the rate of cooling will slow down as the difference between the temperature of the cooling body and the ambient temperature converges. What this means in practical terms is that more scent will be apparent when the surrounding atmosphere is cold, with a relatively warm game bird in it. Add in a steady wind to carry the scent away, and the result will be the most favourable scenting conditions: a steady wind will carry the scent without it dispersing too randomly, whereas a brisk breeze or windy, blustery conditions will break up and disperse the scent more rapidly, and are most likely to give rise to the least favourable conditions for the questing dog.

Under what conditions is this steady wind likely to prevail? Watch the weather forecast and hope they're right! But it is important to consider not only the weather on the large country-wide scale as dictated by large weather system(s), but also the local weather conditions, in which local geography, topography and terrain are the dominant influences. A hill, for example, will force an upward air movement, which cools moisture-laden air sufficiently for it to deposit it as rain – but once the hill is past, the air descends, warms and the rain stops. Thus, so-called 'microclimates' are responsible for local freak weather events that may be at odds with the general forecast.

In valleys, diurnal wind effects are caused as the sun heats the ridges, first creating an upward movement of air; then as the sun goes down, the ridges cool more quickly than the now warm air at the bottom, and a net downward movement of air results, taking the scent with it.

Flat ground will cause even heating and a wholesale upward movement of air, which, coupled with low pressure systems (= unstable air masses, upward-moving, drawing in air) provides the ideal conditions for a steady wind. With high pressure systems (high pressure = highly stable air masses moving downwards, causing the pressure to rise and adiabatic heating) there is reduced likelihood of air movement – and therefore less scent.

Even with the latter conditions of high pressure and no wind, there is some hope. Firstly, during the shooting season the temperatures are relatively low, and as the bird is relatively warm, this creates promising conditions for scent to be imparted to the atmosphere. Air movement, though, is usually thought of as the movement of the air across terrain, but there is another movement, namely that of the bird. We have seen that the pheasant, in particular, is a very alert animal which will, by preference, run as fast and as far as it can before taking to wing. The racket caused by a shooting party, and not least the noise created in the crop by a quartering dog, will be enough to encourage the local resident pheasant population to trot off rapidly in the opposite direction. But it is the very action of running that now provides the airflow over the pheasant which becomes the scent carrier, the scented air hanging, unmoving, just above the ground just at dog nose height. A quartering dog will gleefully pick the scent of the bird up, and, drinking it in, sense that it is a residual scent left by the fleeing quarry, and encouraged, will redouble its efforts in the knowledge that there is certainly game ahead.

Game over? Could be. But we've already seen earlier that one of the game bird's principal defences is stillness. Absence of movement minimizes scent being imparted to the air, which brings us back beautifully to the game bird's paradox: move and give the game away (no pun intended), or keep still. But as we have already seen, stillness is no defence against a capable HPR.

## THE FLUSH

With the dog on point, the next thing to do is to get up close to it in order to control the flush. It is important not to approach the dog from directly behind it: rather, move out wider and approach the dog more from the side so that it can detect your nearing presence out of the corner of its eye. But no matter how far away you may be, do *not* run. Walk briskly. Running creates much more noise as you move through the crop, and this, along with ground vibration, may well unsettle the dog enough for it to dive in and flush the bird before you want it to, or it may unsettle the bird enough so that it decides to go somewhere else and flies off with the poor dog left watching the departure. Neither scenario is the required outcome, and is a lost opportunity for the dog, which had worked hard to find the game for you. As you walk towards the dog you will take those with a gun with you – one, usually two, but up to four – indicating to them where they should position themselves.

Approach the dog slowly, moving in from the side to be next to its head. With the dog on a staunch point it won't move; if it *does* move its head slightly, this is an indication that the bird has moved while you were getting up to the dog. Move your hand down slowly until it is level with the dog's ear but about a foot or two from it, then move it forwards to just in front of the dog, and gently click the fingers, encouraging the dog to move forwards on to the bird. It is amazing that the rigid fixation of the point can so simply be transformed by an innocuous snap of your fingers into the explosive release of poised, concentrated tension propelling it so quickly, so powerfully that the bird barely has time to resort to its primal survival instict… and fly. If it doesn't move, keep doing it but now more urgently. If there is still no movement, use the voice to tell it to 'Get in', which is usually enough to get the dog to break the point, move forwards quickly and drive the bird into the air.

### Sticky Flush

A dog is termed 'sticky' if it flushes hesitantly, or not at all, even with much urging. It is an irritating fault that can be difficult to cure.

### Flushing Too Hard

It is a good thing for the dog, when commanded, to go in fast and flush the bird into the air. Some dogs, though, will go in so hard and fast that the bird hasn't got time to get into the air and is caught instead by the dog: this is called 'pegging the bird'. It can also happen that even if the bird escapes upwards, the dog is going so fast it can't stop, and ends up jumping after the long and very tempting tail feathers. All of which encourages the dog to do things other than what it is supposed to do, which is to sit. This is often the province of the young, enthusiastic dog that

will calm down as it gets older (wishful thinking…?). It may also be moderated by not using the voice command 'get in', or by using it more softly: a loud *'Get in!'* will encourage it to go in harder.

### Sitting to Flush/Shot

With the flush successfully completed, the dog now has to stop or sit and watch the bird fly away. There are two main reasons for this: firstly, the guns will be waiting for the bird to lift so they can attempt a shot at it. It may lift at a steep upward angle so that a gun aiming at it will also be pointing upwards, with the subsequent discharge of shot going safely away (from the point of view of those on the ground – not the bird), but it may well fly away forwards just above the crop, gaining little height. In this case, the guns will be pointing forwards and downwards

*The flush – a German shorthaired pointer flushes a pheasant.*

*A German wirehaired pointer retrieving nicely to hand.*

in the first instance, and it is therefore a highly dangerous place for a dog to be if it happened to chase the bird, and it is precisely this situation that is the most tempting for the dog to start chasing. Secondly, a sitting dog can better mark the fall of shot game; and lastly, it is less likely to 'run in' (retrieve without command). Training should instil in the dog the automatic response to sit when the bird flushes, when it hears the whirring of wings. It may also need the stop whistle or a shout – but whatever signal you need to make, the bum must hit the ground and stay there!

Sitting to shot is essentially that the dog stops or sits, and looks in the direction of the report. It will already have the idea that a shot is likely to result in a falling bird and a retrieve, so it will look to mark the fall – and it can't do this easily when on the move. Whether or not it has marked the fall, it will then look at you for the next command, which could be to retrieve the

marked fall, or a direction command to initiate the blind retrieve of an unmarked fall, or even the recall, depending on the situation (perhaps another dog has been sent), as well as the 'Seek on' command to resume hunting.

## THE RETRIEVE

The final task for the dog is the retrieve of a fallen bird. This is most easily accomplished when the dog has seen the bird come down and has been able to 'Mark' the point of fall. The simple 'Fetch' command is all that should be necessary to start the dog running fast and directly to its mark, when it will find the bird, pick it up and bring it back quickly, delivering it undamaged to hand. It is important that the bird is brought to hand, because it may be still alive and might well run or fly off if the dog simply dumps it down somewhere in front of you. Such

*Directing to a blind retrieve is done with hand signals.*

birds, commonly called 'runners', must be despatched quickly, and the dog must deliver them promptly to you. It should also deliver the bird to you as it found it – a damaged bird, apart from not being very appealing to look at, cannot be sold or put on the dinner table.

A good HPR is capable of finding game unaided, even if it has not been seen to fall over many hundreds of yards, or has come down in water, and sometimes out of sight of the handler; the dog will be gone for as long as it takes – five to ten minutes is not unusual, and an HPR can cover an enormous distance in that time – before reappearing proudly with its prize. Dogs do know when they've done a good job, but we should always tell them, and make a fuss of them when the job is well done.

### Seen Retrieve

This is the simplest retrieve, where the dog has marked the fall and should have no difficulty in quickly executing the retrieve to hand. With multiple falls, the dog should be commanded which one to retrieve first, and subsequently. For example, a runner should always be retrieved promptly and dealt with before any other retrieves are attempted.

## *Blind Retrieve*

Any retrieve that is not a 'seen' retrieve is termed a 'blind retrieve', where the dog has little or no idea of where the bird has fallen. If the handler, gun or anyone else has been able to mark the general whereabouts of the fall, if not the exact spot, the handler will indicate with his hand the direction in which the dog should go, and send it off. Ideally, the dog will run out in a straight line in the direction indicated until it either finds the game or is directed by the handler to do something else: the handler can direct the dog left, right, further back or towards him by means of whistle and hand signals, and when he believes the dog is close to the area in which the retrieve is to be found, will indicate this to the dog using the 'Hi Lost!' command, which will cause it to start hunting around that area for the find.

Knowledge of the wind direction will help the handler to position the dog downwind of the retrieve in order that it has the best chance of picking up the scent in the area. Of course, if the handler really has little idea of where it is, then a successful retrieve is up to the skill and talent of the dog. Retrieving techniques are covered in more detail later.

## *Runners and Pricked Birds*

A runner is a bird that has been shot, but is not yet dead. It could be damaged in some way, for instance with a broken wing, or it may simply be stunned temporarily. Whatever the case, the bird is seen to fall to the ground, but then gets up and runs towards the nearest cover. The pricked bird, by contrast, has been seen to have been shot, but not sufficiently for it to come down immediately: it may be seen to fly or glide on with its wings set, sometimes for a considerable distance. Such birds may be found later by a dog if they happen upon it.

Sometimes the gun swears on his mother's life that he shot the bird stone dead, but come the retrieve the dog is unable to find it in the area indicated, but disappears to come back with the bird that had obviously run off after it had come down.

## *Damaged Game*

Game can become damaged through a variety of causes: shot, fall, the dog, or a combination of all these. This state of affairs is undesirable because the shoot may wish to sell the shot game to a game dealer, who will usually not be interested in taking anything other than freshly shot birds in perfect condition; he will not take damaged birds, or if he does, it will be for nothing – the price per bird to a dealer being ridiculously low in the main – but many shoots take whatever they can get for the day's bag, to reinvest in more corn for the feeders, for example.

### Shot Damage

This is caused by the bird being shot at too close a range, so that it sustains substantial damage to the carcass. This is unlikely to happen on a driven shoot where the birds are going to be presented to the guns at a good height, but it can happen when shooting at a bird flushed by an HPR. The guns arranged around a bird being held by a dog on point will be ten to fifteen yards away – in other words, very close – and it can be very tempting to loose off a shot at the bird as soon as it lifts from being flushed, therefore shooting it at too short a range and resulting in damage to the bird. Guns inexperienced in shooting over HPRs are often guilty of this, being too keen to get the bird on the ground, rather than waiting for it to reach a reasonable distance and become a sporting shot. It does take some nerve to wait as the bird goes away.

### Fall Damage

This is damage sustained by the fall of the bird and could be, for example, damage caused by falling through a tree or by the force of its impact with the ground, or both.

*Retrieving from deep cover can sometimes be difficult.*

## Dog Damage

Damage that can be laid at the door of the dog can be caused by what is termed 'hard mouth', and by damage sustained by the nature of the retrieve. Hard mouth is used to describe the damage sustained when a dog uses unnecessary force with its mouth in the retrieve, and can be detected by feeling the ribcage. It can be caused by sloppy retrieving: a dog that messes about with a bird, trying to find a good grip, or by putting it down on the way back to adjust its grip, can unwittingly do damage, as can a dog that is sent to retrieve a 'runner' – a bird that has been lightly shot, still very much alive but unable to fly, yet able to run, and sometimes very strongly.

A dog sent to retrieve such a bird may be in for a tussle: anyone who has handled pheasant in the pen can testify that they can do serious damage to you with their sharply taloned, scrabbling feet, and you would certainly never contemplate bringing a pheasant anywhere near your face – but this is exactly what the dog has to do, and it is perhaps not surprising if it exerts that little bit more pressure, which stops the bird kicking, scratching and flapping but in doing so causes damage to it. The younger dog may put up with this, but the older one, knowing what it's in for, may well give it that extra sly nip for an easier life.

A dog is deemed to have a hard mouth when it consistently brings back damaged birds and when it is obvious, over a period of time, that the damage is definitely the dog's fault. Unfortunately it is something that cannot be resolved once the habit has embedded itself in the dog's mind. Some HPR breeds are more prone to hard mouth than others, but thankfully most are blessed with a gentle, soft mouth and it is rarely a problem.

## Difficult Retrieve

There may be circumstances where the dog has a difficult time extricating the bird from where it has ended up. If it is in thick bramble, for example, the dog may have a very tough time dragging the retrieve out of the pricking tangle, which may well result in some damage to the bird. This can happen to even the most soft-mouthed of dogs.

All the HPRs are capable of this level of retrieving. The most capable retriever has the benefit of immense talent, and intelligence from its breeding supplemented by months, and even years of dedicated training.

# Chapter 6

# Basic Training

Gundogs are by their nature not difficult to train for experienced dog trainers. For those who have not trained a dog before, it is not recommended that you do it by yourself – the experience of a trainer will enable you to progress with training your pup, it will take the uncertainty out of whether you are doing it correctly, and will be invaluable when things do not go according to plan. With any young dog, the unexpected is never far away, but the experienced trainer will have seen it all before and will be able to guide you as to how to react and correct your dog.

If you are new to training you will probably not be aware that the voice – its pitch, tone and loudness – is used by the experienced trainer to convey pleasure and displeasure: this is really best learned from someone who can demonstrate how it should be done. Find a class that will teach basic obedience – your local vet will

*It's more fun training with others in a group.*

be able to put you in touch with a group, and it will save you a lot of time and trouble. Going to obedience classes is highly beneficial as it will also socialize your dog with others. The techniques that follow are intended for your reference, to understand the basic principles, and as a guide to prepare you for the work ahead; but please – go to a class. You will be expected to practise what you have learned at home, and it is important to do your homework.

If you are planning to go on and work your dog in the field, by all means go to the obedience classes to get the basics in place, but then move on to gundog work with an HPR training group. Paradoxically, too much obedience training is not good for the working HPR, which needs to be able to think for itself, to be more reliant on its instincts and able to work away on its own, with minimal input from you – and over-training can easily compromise these qualities.

## BASIC TRAINING TECHNIQUES AND TIPS

The basics can be started when your pup is about three months old. At this age its attention span will be very short, so keep the sessions correspondingly short, and don't attempt to achieve too much too quickly: the watch words are *little*, but *often*. Treats can be used at this stage, though some people don't believe in their use at all; nevertheless it definitely helps things along in the beginning, but stop using them as soon as you can. They will not be used at all in the more advanced, gundog-specific training. Make the training an enjoyable time for both yourself and the dog: it should feel as if it's a new kind of play – which in a sense it is.

### Correction

When things don't go according to plan, with the dog not obeying or messing about, you need to let it know that it is not doing the right thing. Conversely, when it does something well, praise it effusively. It is important that you convey your pleasure or displeasure, such that the dog is in absolutely no doubt, immediately – a dog only associates your praise or otherwise with the last thing it was doing, and for example, if you don't intervene while it is still engaged in the unwanted act, it will have moved on to something else, and you will have missed the moment – you will now be berating the dog for what it is engaged in *now*, and not what it *was* engaged in. A classic problem that illustrates this, is when the dog runs in and retrieves a bird or dummy without being told to do so: it runs off on its own initiative (which you *don't* want it to do), gets to the retrieve, picks it up nicely (which you *do* want it to do) and brings it back nicely to hand (which you do also want it to do). You can't berate it for correctly picking up the bird, or bringing it back to hand, but you do want to berate it for going off before you told it to. The only chance for correction is to yell at the dog when it sets off, or if you can head it off before it reaches the retrieve.

Correction can be a simple 'Ah, Ah!' or 'No!', with varied degrees of loudness and a sense of anger in the voice, or physical correction for more serious transgressions. One of the most effective methods is to grab hold of the dog with a hand on each side of the scruff of the neck, and lift it up so that all four legs are off the ground; then look it directly in the eyes and say 'No, no, no!' or 'What do you think you are doing?!' – and put it down again. A dog doesn't like its feet being off the ground, and the direct eye contact sends it a powerful message.

Wilson Stephens, in his book *Gundog Sense and Sensibility* (1982, Quiller Press), has this to say:

> Given that the element of defiance is identifiable (we can all recognise it, since we encounter it often enough), my objective is to make a mark on the dog's consciousness which will secure compliance in future without reducing its confidence

in me. This is explicitly different from letting off steam or bolstering my outraged ego.

In the process I put no great faith in anything which involves striking the animal. Dogs do not beat each other. When the pack leader quells insubordination he seizes the offender by the lip, the ear or the throat, more rarely by the scruff or the foreleg, and gives it a good shaking. This is the manner in which canine domination is exercised, and I do likewise.

A dog thus grasped by a man is at once in a position of inferiority. If lifted clear of the ground (i.e. parted from its natural element) inferiority is intensified into subservience, embarrassment, even ridicule, of which dogs are sharply conscious. A shaking, demonstrating that anything a dog can do, man can do better, is all that is needed to underline human superiority. This superiority will be related to the offence if it is imposed exactly where the offence occurred, without delay, without anger (though obviously with indications of disapproval), and above all without an intervening act of obedience by the dog, however small.

It is important to be absolutely consistent with correction and praise so there can be no confusion whatever in the dog's mind.

## The Lead

Gundogs in the field don't wear a collar (in case it gets caught up in undergrowth, which would be potentially dangerous), and a slip lead is usually employed. For the pet, when you are in a public place where a collar is in any case mandatory, any lead is fine.

## The Sit

Have a small treat ready in your hand and offer it to the pup, which hopefully will gobble it down and look for more. Get another treat and make sure the pup knows that it's in your hand: this

*Hungarian Vizsla sitting and waiting attentively for the next command.*

way, you already have its attention because its interest is in the treat. Sit on the floor and wait for the pup to come up to you. Tell it to 'Sit' in a normal tone of voice, and at the same time move the hand containing the treat towards the dog's nose, raising your hand so that it moves above its head. The pup's nose will move up as it follows the treat, and as you continue to move your hand further back over its head, the pup will automatically sit. When it does so, say 'Good boy!' (or 'girl'), then hold the treat for a few moments before letting him have it, with lots of praise and a cuddle from you.

Repeat this no more than a couple of times a day, but every day, and very quickly you should be able to say 'Sit' and get an immediate response. When things are starting to work properly, don't give the treat every time, and stop altogether as soon as you can — you don't want to get the pup into the situation where it is *always* looking for a treat.

## The Recall/Come

Sit the dog and back away a few yards. Call the dog to you with 'Come': say it in a light tone and not too loud, there is no need to shout, and at the same time hold out your hands to encourage the dog to come to you; if it hesitates, repeat the command — crouching down will also help. Usually a pup is only too happy to come for a cuddle! Praise it effusively when it arrives. Every day move further and further away. The whistle can be introduced as soon as the pup is coming to your call consistently. Blow 'pip, pip, pip' on the whistle and then call 'Come!' with the voice, and the pup will start to associate the 'pip, pip, pip' with the voice recall — and very soon the whistled recall will start to work on its own. Always praise the dog when it is successful. Effusive praise is easily forgotten, but is so vital in gaining the trust and respect of your dog — don't take it for granted.

*It is very important to instil the 'recall' whistle at an early stage.*

## The Stay

Once the sit is working consistently well we can introduce the stay. Sit the pup, say 'Stay', and move away slowly, facing the pup at all times – don't turn away at this stage. If the pup starts to move, go back towards it (which will help stop its forward movement) saying 'Ah, ah!' by way of correction, then pick it up and take it back to where it should have been sitting, put it down firmly, and repeat. A young dog is easily picked up and replaced where it should be, and holding it by the scruff of the neck will not hurt it.

Only say 'Stay' once, at the beginning: don't get into the habit of saying 'Stay, stay, stay' every few steps as you go backwards. When it is staying put and you can move two to three yards away, walk back to it, and on reaching it, praise it while gently stroking its front. Correct any movement with 'Ah, ah!' Extend this exercise by walking out two to three yards, and then progress by walking in a circle around the dog, moving in occasionally to praise and stroke it. Progressively extend the distance, and recall with praise.

## The Heel

This exercise is best done at a place where there are no distractions such as cars, people or other dogs. Your young dog is easily enough distracted and will be interested in everything apart from what you want it to concentrate on, so make your life a little easier and find somewhere secluded. Walk the dog along with the lead held in your left hand. Say 'Heel!' in a normal voice, and at the same time pull the lead sharply so the dog is pulled up abruptly and back to your side – you won't hurt it, and it is more the surprise that will have the desired effect. This needs to be repeated continuously until eventually you are able to walk along with a loose lead. Don't expect miracles: this will take some time, but

it's a battle you have to win, and you will if you are patient and just persevere. It is important not to get angry or shout at the dog, even when it continues to pull ahead – keep cool, say 'Heel', and yank it back to your side. You need to reserve your angry voice for situations when it has really transgressed and needs to know it; if you always use a loud, angry voice and facial expression the dog will eventually 'tune it out', and the effect will be diminished as it will simply start to ignore you.

## Leave

This can be employed in a number of situations. The pup is going to get its nose into all kinds of new and interesting things, some of which may not be too pleasant or desirable. Fresh horse dung is a favourite but you will find that it becomes less interesting the older it becomes. Eventually, the dog will simply ignore it. Fox droppings are another favourite with a memorable smell and you'll need to react quickly when you see a shoulder on the way down to have a nice roll. Chase it off – you do need to get your running shoes on – calling 'Leave'. If it happens to be on the lead when this happens, so much the better, because you can give it a light tug along with the command 'Leave' to gently encourage it away. The command is extended for the working gundog, as we shall see later.

## Problems

It would be impossible to cover all possible remedies to problems that arise in training, besides which there are often many solutions to a particular problem. Remember that many of the problems that are exhibited by the dog may well stem from handler error or mistakes in training, particularly with inexperienced trainers and those new to gundogs. The plea, to be emphasized yet again, is to make sure you go to a training class for HPR dogs.

*German shorthaired pointer pointing grouse on the moors.*

## GUNDOG TRAINING

Now you have the basics in place you may not feel the need to carry on with any further training, but are happy to enjoy your HPR as a family companion. But if you want to use your dog in the shooting field, or to compete at field trials or working tests, then further specialized gundog training is required. It is worth pointing out that further training is good for the dog, and it will enjoy the mental challenges, the attention and the training environment outdoors with the opportunity to socialize with others. The owner, likewise, may well equally enjoy the challenges, and will take pride in what the dog can be trained to do.

Many enjoy attending the weekly training class, with no intention or desire to take to the shooting field, but many do enjoy exercising their skills at the gundog events that take place out of season: the spring and grouse pointing and the working tests, all of which are extremely popular, particularly the working tests, which take place throughout the summer months. Working tests are described in detail in Chapter 8.

It cannot be emphasized enough that successful training of your gundog is best done with experienced HPR trainers, either one-to-one or in a group. HPRs are unique in their all-round capability, and the way they carry out their tasks is simply different to other gundog breeds, so it follows that their training will also be different. There are close similarities, for example in retrieving, but the differences are important even if sometimes subtle: for instance, an HPR does not retrieve in the same way as other breeds of retrieving dogs, the chief difference being the way the HPR will use the wind – which is not to say that it is in any way inferior, just that it will do it slightly differently. Those who work and train HPRs know how to get the very best out of them, and will be happy to pass on their knowledge and experience to you; so it is important to go to the specialist (it won't cost any more) and get it right to start with.

Even those who are very experienced HPR handlers, and successfully train their own dogs, value such groups: it helps to have more people and dogs around, as a young dog will learn by watching others, and socializing your dog is always a good thing; also you need to have dummy throwers, someone to fire the dummy launcher and to put out blind retrieves, all of which can be done most conveniently in turn by those in the group. And it's more fun. You will have your homework to do between sessions, which you will need to do on your own, but you will find it a relief to go back to the group the following week to sort out the problems you encountered in the meantime.

Gundog training takes a lot of time and commitment. From pup to fully trained dog it takes about two to three years, depending on the dog – as with humans, dogs mature at different rates, some are more intelligent than others, some are quick learners. Don't let the length of time put you off. In the first place, there is no way round it – it just takes this long. Second, it is the most rewarding journey for you and your dog.

With HPRs, the training elements described below start at about six months, and there is a logical progression that follows on from the basic training: you can't teach 'stay' until 'Sit' works, and you can't teach steadiness until the stop whistle is working. It is very easy to push your dog along too quickly, especially with HPRs that can learn quickly, so you feel you can move on to the next stage. You may be right, but it is all too easy to fall into the trap of doing too much, usually by having training sessions that go on too long. Remember: little, but often. Overtraining can have the effect of making the sessions feel like a chore for you and the dog, and rather than looking forward to a fun time, you could have a dog thoroughly fed up with the whole thing – in extreme cases the dog may just refuse to do anything. If this does happen, simply stop all training for a month.

### The Whistle Commands

Indispensable to any gundog handler, the whistle is your remote control unit, powered by a renewable energy source: your breath. Don't leave home without it. Equip yourself with an ACME 210 1/2 or 211 1/2, available from any gundog supplier – the difference is in the pitch of the whistle, the choice being essentially your personal preference. Elementary acoustic physics will tell you that high frequencies require more energy to generate, and are attenuated more quickly: that is, they don't travel as far as lower-pitched sounds, those at a lower frequency. However, all dog whistles are designed to operate within the most sensitive part of the dog's aural frequency spectrum. Once you've decided which one you prefer, you should stick with it. A dog's hearing is extremely acute, and can tell the difference between two 210 1/2 whistles blown by the same person – they may sound the same to us, but not to a dog. And if we humans can recognize the whistling characteristics of another handler in the group, you can bet the dog can. Whistle commands are:

*'Acme' whistle.*

| Short pip: | Pay attention, look at me for the next command (usually a hand signal) |
| Pip, pip: | Change direction |
| Pip, pip, pip: | Recall or come towards the handler |
| Long whistle: | Stop and sit |

Blown very gently so that the whistle barely makes a noise acts as a low-key stop signal, and can be used to slow the dog down to a stop; it is also used when approaching a dog on point in order to reinforce steadiness. Start to use the whistle very early on in training. For example, most young dogs tend not to go too far away from you, reaching a certain distance before looking back or running back to you. When they start to run back to you, blow the recall 'pip pip pip' – it won't understand what this means, but it will progressively begin to associate coming back to you with the whistle.

When your dog is off the lead, always have the whistle in your mouth ready for action. It is absolutely useless to have it dangling somewhere in front of you (even worse if you've zipped up your fleece, trapping the whistle inside) when you need to stop the dog *now*: fumbling for precious seconds can be crucial. So always have it constantly in your mouth, or at least in your hand so it can be brought into immediate use.

### Other Equipment

Apart from a gundog slip lead (get a couple at least), you will need a puppy dummy, and a couple of 1lb canvas dummies as the bare minimum equipment. A Kong is useful, but not absolutely necessary, for the introduction to water retrieves.

Much of what follows can be done in parallel, or a number of them combined at different times in a session; but it is important that this is done with the progress of the particular dog(s) in mind – and it is best for this to be done by an experienced trainer, and another good reason to be in an HPR training class.

### Gundog Recall

While the recall to voice may be sufficient for a pet, the gundog needs to respond to the whistle. The basic recall was covered earlier, and we just need to reinforce the response for the gundog. The three pips will bring the dog back to you, but a good refinement is to make the dog sit at your side, which is quite easily achieved if you insist on it sitting whenever it comes back to you – every time, without exception.

While it is good training practice to use the recall whistle often – and with a hard-running dog, very often – do bear in mind that it can also have the effect of limiting the distance the dog goes away from you: if every time you recall you do so when the dog is fifty yards from you, it will start to think that fifty yards is as far as it is allowed to go, and no further. With a dog that you are trying to encourage to range out further from you, the over-use of the recall can undo all the good work; in such cases you should therefore avoid using the recall as much as possible – quite often the dog that is reluctant to range out too far is uncertain, and will respond all too readily to the recall as it immediately puts it back in its comfort zone near to you – so try to leave it alone.

## The Leave

We use 'Leave' or 'Leave that' as an adjunct to steadiness. It is also employed when the dog presents the retrieve to you, to instruct it to release its grip in order for you to take the retrieve from it (some people use 'Dead', though it doesn't really matter as long as you are consistent). Use it if the dog spots something that it is obviously thinking about chasing, such as a hare, rabbit or deer. You might also use it just before throwing a dummy, to reinforce steadiness.

## Steadiness

We tend to labour steadiness, as it is fundamental to the good working of the shooting dog. A dog that runs in, or is not steady to shot, is at risk and will be a nuisance on the shooting field; it will also be eliminated at a field trial, and will record a zero at working tests. These are all good reasons to really ensure that your dog is steady in all circumstances.

### Exercise 1
A useful warm-up before you start to do anything else in a session is to sit your dog, move away a few yards, and then throw a series of dummies around it and over its head. Saying 'Leave' before you throw helps to reinforce the steadiness when you first start on this exercise. This works well with a group: sit the dogs in a circle, and the handlers throw dummies in all directions – in front of the dogs and over their heads. When all the dummies have been thrown,

*Throwing dummies around a dog is a great way of training steadiness.*

don't let the dogs pick any of them: the handlers should do that; then repeat the exercise. It is a good plan not to allow a dog always to have a retrieve: it sends a powerful message to the dog if you go and pick up the dummy yourself, so do it now and then throughout its training.

If any of the dogs breaks from the sit, shout 'Ah, *ah!*', move quickly to catch it and bring it back, by the scruff of the neck, to the exact position that it was in, and sit it again.

### Exercise 2

All retrieving practice is also an exercise in steadiness, as the dog is required to watch dummies being thrown, only retrieving them on command. It is good practice to make the dog wait longer than usual before sending it off for the retrieve, particularly if the dog does not have its rear fully on the ground, but hovering and ready to go – make it sit properly, and extend the wait for a few moments more.

### Exercise 3

A good exercise that combines sitting to shot as well as steadiness is to simulate a beating line by arranging a class of dogs with handlers spread out along a line. A helper carrying a dummy launcher is positioned at one end of the line. With the dogs off the lead and walking to heel, the line is advanced forwards. When the dummy launcher is fired, all dogs should sit to the report. One dog is then sent for the retrieve.

*'Stop' whistle – make sure you get this working perfectly.*

## The Stop/Sit to Whistle

Sitting (also known as 'dropping') to the whistle is the most fundamental and important function to be ingrained in your dog. It is, in fact, quite easy to teach the very young dog while out on its walk; it is useful to walk your dog to heel for a while, you stop and it sits. Now, when you stop and the dog automatically starts to sit, gently blow the stop whistle. In this way, the dog begins to make the association between stop, sit, and the whistle. Very soon you will be able to blow gently on the whistle, and the dog will sit. Keep doing this whenever you walk the dog.

Having got the dog to sit to whistle beside you, we now need to move on and teach the dog to sit wherever it happens to be when the stop whistle is sounded. There are a number of methods, but if the recall is working, use this: when the dog is a little way in front you, blow the recall, and as soon as it is on its way back towards you, blow the stop whistle and run towards the dog with your right arm raised – this has the effect of surprising it, and it is highly likely that the dog will look at you as though you've lost your mind, but eventually it will sit. Praise it. Repeat this once or twice a day, and eventually it will sit to whistle wherever it happens to be. While walking on the lead, a good reinforcement exercise is to stop, and blow the whistle gently to make it sit.

## The Sit to Shot

It is important to instil in the dog the notion of sitting as soon as a gunshot or report is heard. The reasons are covered later in Chapter 10 on field trials so they won't be repeated here, but this a basic requirement for a gundog. It is useful to have access to, or to own, a starting pistol and a dummy launcher – though if you don't own one, don't worry, someone in your HPR training group will have one. Remember that with a young dog that has not experienced the sound of a shotgun it can by spooked or frightened by a loud bang in close proximity, which is a situation that we want to avoid. Make sure that the pistol or launcher is well away from the dog before it is activated – twenty-five yards or so to start with. Walk the dog on the lead with the helper armed with the starting pistol walking some distance away but keeping abreast. At your signal, the pistol is fired, and at this very moment pull back the lead sharply and say '*Sit*'. The dog may well jump around to locate the source of the sound, but you must insist on it sitting.

Repeat the exercise until the dog has made the association between the sound of the pistol and the requirement on its part to sit, at which point the pull on the lead should no longer be necessary. This exercise can also be done with a number of dogs – and even if you are not the handler currently being walked up the field, do not lose the opportunity to reinforce these lessons by keeping your dog standing and making it sit on the sound of the pistol. It may be that the dummy launcher is being used for retrieving, and again, use the opportunity to reinforce the sit to shot as previously.

Once this is working well, the next step is to get the dog to sit to shot or whistle wherever it happens to be – especially when out hunting. It is easier to get the dog to stop running and sit when it is going away from you so pre-arrange this with whoever is firing the pistol or launcher for you. If you are using a dummy launcher, arrange it to be fired in such a direction that the dog has to pass in front of you if it were to set off after the dummy, ignoring the shot and your stop whistle – this way, you have a chance of getting yourself between the dog and the dummy in an effort to stop it.

## The Sit to Flush

We have already discussed sitting to shot, and also the requirement to sit when the bird lifts following the flush. Now, as we come to introduce the dog to game, it is also the time to train the dog in this aspect. Even out of season it is perfectly possible for your dog to come across a game bird and point it. Don't let it flush a bird it might point, but use the opportunity to reinforce the staunchness of the point: move up slowly to the side of your dog, as we've previously discussed, alert for any sign of it moving, and blow your whistle gently if you think it necessary. When you are up to it, it will help to stroke the dog along it's back while gently saying 'Good boy', and being close up to the dog puts you in a good position to hold it steady with your free hand if it seems as though it may be tempted to move.

Slip the lead on, and gently lead it away if you don't want it to flush the bird. However, now you are more in control you can encourage it to go forwards and flush the bird: keep moving forwards until the bird flushes, using the lead to stop the dog moving forward and vocal encouragement to sit as the bird flies away. Make sure the dog is sitting, and leave it sitting quietly for a few seconds with you. Then let it off the lead and allow it to explore the area where the bird lifted so that it can drink in the scent.

Under no circumstances should the dog be allowed to flush off the lead until you are fairly confident that it will sit to the flush and will not chase. Of course, there is never a guarantee, even with an experienced dog, that this will not happen, and if it does, make sure at once that the dog knows it has erred.

### Retrieving: Starting Off

Often the pup will start to bring you things from around the house without any bidding from you: a slipper will arrive, a bit of firewood, a handbag, all of which should be highly praised: let the dog know it's doing the right thing, and never chastise it – after all, the dog is not to know that the handbag is hugely expensive. With some dogs, this phase never goes away.

You can start the pup retrieving in the home, in the kitchen or living room: simply throw a toy, and praise the pup when it comes back to you with it – really exaggerate the praise. Don't worry if it plays around with the toy and doesn't bring it back to you immediately, and don't admonish it, because eventually there will be an opportunity for you to throw the toy again – what we are trying to establish is a simple game that the pup enjoys, so no pressure and keep it fun. Gradually, after a day or so when the toy comes back for another go, make the pup sit and hold it gently by the scruff of the neck so it can't run forwards, and throw the toy with your free hand. Keep it sitting a moment longer, then let it go with the word 'Fetch' or 'Fetch it'. Now we are starting to introduce steadiness and the notion of retrieving to command, and it's still a game – playing tug with it won't hurt, either.

Introduce the puppy dummy, but remove it from the dog's mouth as soon as it comes back to you with the word 'Leave' or 'Dead' (whichever you want, but choose one and stick with it), and don't let the pup have it again until the next day. Continue to play with another toy, by all means. The idea here is to impress upon the dog that the puppy dummy comes straight back to you, that this dummy is special, it's yours, and not to be played with.

For the next stage, try to find a path or similar, somewhere that has defined boundaries so that the dog can run up and down the lane but not off elsewhere – paths through woods are good for this. The reason for this is that the dog can't run off with the dummy – it could run away from you, but puppies generally don't, and it has to come back to you. Plus, there is no scope for running past you – it has to come up to you, and you should be able to block its way easily if you think it is going to run past you. In open fields there is endless scope for the dog to run off or run around you with the dummy, refusing to come near. Don't attempt to start training in the open until the dog has been to such a location enough to be used to it. And don't stop the games at home – they should continue for a while longer.

*Paths in woods are perfect for initial retrieving.*

One day, call the dog to you, sit it down, and throw a dummy just a short distance away, saying 'Leave that' just before you throw – try to make sure the dog doesn't run to fetch it, but don't worry too much if it does – and send it for the dummy by saying 'Back'. At the start only do this once a day to keep up the pup's enthusiasm; even if it looks at you, and obviously wants another go, put the dummy in your pocket and continue the walk – this has the effect of reinforcing the notion in the dog's mind that the dummy is yours, and being allowed to retrieve it is a privilege that you control.

The dog should become steady to the throw of the dummy if you say 'Leave' just before the throw, and are ready to stop it running forwards by holding on to the scruff of its neck, and later, when it stops pulling, by holding your hand in front of its chest so that you can quickly stop it if it tries to run forwards. If the dog does look as if it's going to break, say 'Leave!' or 'No!' firmly. With persistent offenders, catch the dog as it starts to break – it's not difficult

if you are anticipating it and are ready – hold it by the scruff, haul it back to where it should be sitting and firmly re-position it with the command 'Sit and stay!' If the dog manages to run forwards you can shout 'No!', blow the stop whistle, and shout *What do you think you are doing?'* – anything verbal to get it to stop. If you can't, and it is obvious it's going to get the retrieve, let it have it. We don't want to tell it off for retrieving.

After a few days, when you are happy that this exercise is working well, extend the distance progressively, say by twenty yards, and then another twenty. If the dog hesitates at the new distance, encourage it on the outrun with 'Go on, go on!'; if it is still hesitant, then move quickly forwards – don't let it come back towards you. Reduce the distance and consolidate before attempting to stretch it again. Be happy if you can achieve thirty to forty yards – you won't need any more for the first year, but if you can keep increasing the distance, this is all to the good. What you don't want to do is to have it retrieving at the

## The Dummy Launcher

A dummy launcher is a device that throws a dummy a hundred yards or so, and works by firing a blank cartridge in the body of the launcher. Its big advantage is that it throws the dummy a far greater distance than you could possibly throw, and thereby creates a more challenging retrieve. Make sure you hold the launcher correctly: if you hold it with your thumb against the launcher body, you will regret it! Many find that the launcher shoulder butt is a convenient device that is more comfortable to use. The launcher will make a very loud bang so it is essential to wear hearing protection.

*Holding the launcher correctly — like this — is very important to avoid injury.*

*If you hold the thumb against the launcher body like this, the recoil will hurt it.*

*Pushing the dummy half way down the spigot reduces the distance it is thrown.*

Be aware that a dog can become accustomed to the range of the launcher and, knowing this, will happily trot out to the distance it knows it will find the dummy, and won't go any further. To avoid this conditioning becoming embedded, position the person with the launcher further and further forwards so as to increase the total distance. Also, it is useful to vary the direction of the launch, not always straight ahead in an effort to gain the maximum retrieve distance, but out to the left and right and all points between, which will aid the dog's ability to mark the point of fall.

When starting with a dog new to the launcher, it is advantageous to push the dummy half-way down the spigot on the launcher because this has effect of reducing the distance that the dummy will be thrown.

The angle at which the launcher is held determines the distance the dummy is thrown; hold it parallel to the ground and the dummy's flight is most easily seen by the dog, bouncing and rolling as it lands. This is the method that is the most tempting for the dog, and so will test its steadiness. After this method has been used and the dog is able to retrieve consistently, the launcher can be progressively angled upwards. This is more difficult as the dog may not see the flight of the dummy or its fall, with the possibility of its being asked to make an unintended 'blind' retrieve, which may be beyond its capability.

It is a good idea when training with the launcher to say 'Mark' or 'Watch' just before the launcher is fired to gain the attention of the dog so that it is looking in the direction of the launcher. If it isn't, it is highly unlikely that it will see the dummy in flight – it's a very small thing to see at a distance, and virtually impossible to pick up visually once it is on its way. Dogs do have a habit of looking away at the critical moment before launch, and the verbal reminder really helps to get them looking in the right direction.

*Many find the shoulder butt is more comfortable and convenient to use.*

same distance all the time, because you run the real risk of this distance being so ingrained in the dog's mind that it won't go any further. Later on, with blind retrieving, you set the dog off in a particular direction and need it to keep going until you tell it otherwise, so you must not 'teach' it that a dummy is always to be found at forty yards, as it may be fifty or 150.

While extending the distance, mix in a new exercise: sit the dog, throw the dummy, and then walk the dog, to heel, away from the dummy for ten yards, turn round, sit the dog, and then send it for the retrieve. This is the simple memory retrieve.

### The Simple Seen Retrieve

For the simple seen retrieve a helper is positioned about twenty-five yards in front of you and your dog. They will make a loud noise, clap the hands over the head with the dummy so the dog's attention is engaged, and throw the dummy to one side. Throwing it upwards makes it easier for the dog to see the flight and mark the fall. The dog should be steady, only going to retrieve the dummy when commanded; the steadiness exercises can be used to reinforce this discipline if necessary. As the dog becomes more proficient and confident at this distance, gradually extend it. Don't be tempted to make large changes of distance, as young dogs have a tendency to mark short – that is, they see the fall of the dummy and mentally mark the distance to it, but as their perception of distance is immature they actually run to a point short of the retrieve and start to look for it. Increasing the distance gradually will help the dog to

*Clearly indicate the direction of the retrieve with an outstretched arm.*

interpret correctly what it sees, to distance over the ground.

### 'Mark' and 'Watch'

The words 'Mark' or 'Watch' can be used just before the throw of a dummy, or just before the dummy launcher is fired, to gain the dog's attention and gradually build the association between the word and the appearance of a retrieve in flight. It is important that the dog watches the dummy right from the start of its flight, because it must follow its trajectory and mentally note – mark – the point of fall. It is most useful with the younger dog, which quite often shows interest in everything else around it, rather than doing what you want, which is to sit still and pay attention to your helper whooping away in the distance. Dogs seem to have an unfailing tendency – particularly when the dummy launcher is employed – of being distracted by something which causes them to look away just at the critical moment of the thing going off: the bang makes them look to the sound, but by then it's too late and the dummy has already flown.

Stretching your arm out in the direction of the helper or dummy launcher and saying 'Mark' or 'Watch' can gain the dog's attention at the critical moment. If the bee, butterfly, or whatever is distracting its attention is still more interesting than your 'Mark', use your hand to move its head back to the front and say 'Mark' more sternly.

### *Presenting the Retrieve*

The retrieve should always end with the dog bringing the dummy or bird to your hand, and not dumping it down a yard in front of you. It is always a nice finish to a retrieve when the dog sits in front of you, head up, offering the game to you. This is known as the 'present'. Some owners and handlers insist on the dog always presenting in this way, no matter what the occasion or what has been retrieved. Others only insist on dummies being presented this way, any

retrieved game being delivered to hand without any more fuss or ceremony. In the latter case this makes sense, because the training dummy weighs a mere 1lb, whereas the average pheasant weighs in at around 2–3½lb, and this is a lot more for the dog to have to carry, sometimes a considerable distance, over obstacles, or even from water when it will weigh even more. Under these circumstances, you are just happy that the dog has done its job well in getting it back to you, and it is almost an insult to then expect it to present as well. In the working test, however, a dummy nicely presented rounds off the retrieve in a pleasing way.

While it is easier to teach the present to the younger dog, it should first be happy with its retrieving, and consistently delivering to hand. When this is the case, then we can start to work on the present. Start in the garden, by throwing a dummy (a light puppy dummy is fine for starting this off): when the dog comes back to you, pat your stomach with both hands to encourage the dog in close to you – you can encourage it with the words 'Come on, come on' spoken in a gentle, neutral voice. If it won't come closer, move back a step and encourage it to follow, and again if necessary, still patting the stomach. When it is closer to you, say 'Sit', still patting your stomach – this encourages the dog to look up towards your hands, and the closer the dog is to you the more it has to look up. It is now sitting, looking up at you with the retrieve in its mouth – presenting. Bend down slowly and gently stroke the front of its chest for a few moments, saying 'Good boy, good boy', which encourages it to hold the dummy until you finally move your hand to the dummy and say 'Dead', or 'Leave it', when it should be released.

It is unlikely that it will all go as smoothly as this, however, and if it does – and sometimes it can – then count yourself lucky! Often the dog will drop the dummy, rather than holding it in the mouth until you are ready, but this is a battle of wills that you must win. You need to watch for any sign that the dummy is about to

be dropped, anticipate it happening, and as soon as you think it is about to occur say 'Hold it, hold it!' in a stern voice. If the dummy is then dropped, say 'Ah, ah' immediately, to let the dog know that it has done wrong.

If the hold is not improving after a few sessions it may be necessary to put the dummy in the dog's mouth. To do this, pat the underside of the dog's lower jaw saying 'Hold, hold'. Be very careful how you put the dummy into its mouth. Prise the jaws open gently with one hand, making sure that the flews – the flaps of skin on either side of the upper jaw – are folded up away from the teeth before inserting the dummy gently and letting the jaws take grip. If you don't do this the flaps may get caught between the dummy and the upper set of teeth, which will be painful for the dog and will not help your cause – it's hardly going to be happy about holding the dummy for you if it's in pain. Once in, continue to say 'Hold it, hold it' – and 'Ah ah' if it looks like loosening its grip – and praise with 'Good boy' if it continues to hold, perhaps with an encouraging chest stroking, but all the time saying 'Hold it, hold it. Good boy!' and so on. Use 'Ah, ah' immediately if you need to.

When this starts to work, move away from the dog slowly, still intoning 'Hold it, hold it' and praising it if it's doing well. If you can, walk all the way round the dog slowly, all the while saying 'Hold it, hold it', so that it has to rotate its head to follow your movement. While moving around, move back into the dog, stroke it saying 'Good boy, good boy', and move away again. Remember to give a lot of praise if it does this nicely. This may work at the first attempt, or it may need a few sessions with particularly recalcitrant pupils – but work it will, with some perseverance. Don't make these sessions very long, a couple of minutes at most. Remember: little, but often. And don't get angry or shout. Keep your voice gentle and neutral as much as

*OPPOSITE: Perfectly presenting to the handler rounds off a good retrieve and will impress those watching.*

you can – only stern or reproachful when necessary, then immediately reverting to the neutral and encouraging voice.

### Commands Initiating the Retrieve

#### 'Back' and 'Fetch'
The command 'Back' is used to set the dog off in a direction away from us, and is employed when first setting the dog off, or when we need it go further away from us. Different trainers use 'Back', 'Go back', 'Back and fetch' to describe the same action, and you will undoubtedly adopt the command that is used at your particular training class. It doesn't matter which one you choose as long as the same command is used consistently. Many use 'Back and fetch' when setting the dog off on a retrieve, and only use 'Back' as a method of commanding the dog – usually when it is sitting at a distance facing you and waiting for the next command – to turn 180 degrees and run on a line further away from you. The command is usually accompanied by a hand signal; when the dog is a considerable distance away, the hand signal alone is used. Some will use 'Back' in both situations.

The simple seen retrieve is initiated by 'Back' or the 'Fetch' command. It is confusing that both 'Back' and 'Fetch' are used for apparently the same thing: to fetch the retrieve. The essential difference is that 'Back' will tell the dog that it needs to run off in the indicated direction for some way before the retrieve will be found, but 'Fetch' can be used to initiate a seen retrieve. Perhaps in an effort to alleviate any confusion that might arise from this, some use 'Back and fetch'. Occasionally a dog may be hovering over a retrieve instead of picking it up immediately, either because it may be uncertain of the right thing to do, or perhaps because it simply doesn't fancy picking it up. Then, the word 'Fetch' or 'Fetch it' is used to encourage the retrieve. This is often the case when a dog encounters something new, such as a dummy from a launcher

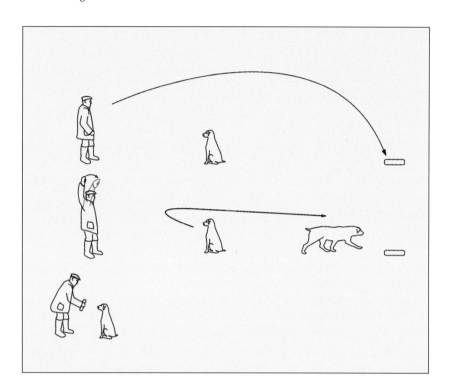

*'Go back!': the forward movement of the hand tells the dog to turn round and go away from the handler.*

that is of a slightly different construction to the dummies it has been used to (some are canvas-covered, other smooth plastic), and which will reek – to the dog – not of human scent through handling, but of the explosive charge residue.

### 'Back' Exercise 1

Sit the dog and, standing a short distance in front of it, throw the dummy over its head so it lands behind it. Raise your right hand so that it is stretched vertically upwards with the open palm of your hand towards the dog. Now quickly move your hand forwards as if you are pushing at something, and at the same time say 'Go back!' Some trainers use 'Back', others 'Back and fetch' – but it doesn't matter what you say, as long as you always say the same thing.

### 'Back' Exercise 2

Here we initiate the retrieve, which is behind the dog, so that it has to go 'Back' for it. At heel, walk the dog fifteen yards forwards, and tell it to sit. Throw the dummy a few yards ahead.

Now be careful, because we want to turn round and walk away: look at the dog hard and say 'Heel' – be ready to catch it if it starts to go for the dummy – then walk away from the dummy for ten yards, with the dog to heel, and then tell it to sit. Now continue walking backwards facing the sitting dog. Stop after ten yards, and hold up your right hand and say *'Back!'*, pushing your hand forwards as you do so. It is to be hoped that the dog will take the cue and run for the retrieve.

It may stay sitting, however, and look confused, in which case walk briskly up to it saying 'Back! back!' If it still doesn't go, walk up to it and set it up for the normal retrieve – don't admonish it, and send it off as you normally would – it is more important to make the retrieve successful and to praise the dog, rather than dwell on the fact that it didn't do it in exactly the right way. Try it again the following day – it will come.

And when this is working satisfactorily, increase the distances progressively.

## The 'Hi Lost!' Command

Quite often the dog will be in the area of the dummy but can't find it immediately, and starts to hunt around. This is the time to introduce the 'Hi lost!' command: as it hunts around, call 'Hi lost, hi lost!' at intervals until it finds the retrieve. After a time, the dog will associate the call with the need to hunt around in a small area, and this is important. Later on, when the dog is out a long way on a blind retrieve, you will direct it by hand signals to where you believe the retrieve is to be found, and as it approaches this area call out 'Hi lost!', which tells the dog it should start hunting in this vicinity. If the dog's hunting takes it out of the area, use the whistle and hand signal to bring it back, and then call 'Hi lost!' again. Repeated success for the dog will teach it to trust the words 'Hi lost', and to make the association between the command and the area to hunt. It's not infallible, though: you may think the retrieve is in a particular area, call 'Hi lost!' – and the dog promptly dives off somewhere else and finds it! So you may need to 'trust your dog' to know what it's doing.

## The 'There!' Command

This command is used when you know the dog is extremely close to the retrieve, and tells it to hunt in a very confined area to locate it – the dog must be almost on top of the retrieve, as far as you can tell, before you use 'There!', otherwise it will not be able to differentiate between the meaning of 'There!' and that of 'Hi lost!'. You would expect to use 'There!' when the scenting conditions are not good, with the dog going over where you think the retrieve is, but not 'winding' it.

It is very important to keep in mind that 'There!' means 'There, right there' and should only ever be used when you are absolutely sure that the dummy or retrieve is actually 'there', and very close indeed. If it is a few yards away, it isn't 'There', so use 'Hi lost' to keep the dog hunting in the vicinity. The way to train 'There' is as follows: when the young dog is running out

to a retrieve, call 'There!' just before it is about to pick it up, so it gradually makes the association between the command and proximity.

## Consolidation at Class

As mentioned above, the track or path through the woods is perfect for starting retrieving, because the dog is less likely to run off willy-nilly. But sooner or later the same exercise needs to be demonstrated on open ground. The training class (you are going to one, aren't you?) is a good place for this, and the most likely situation where your dog will start playing up, since the combination of open ground, the distraction of people, interesting smells and the presence of other dogs, all conspire against you.

## *The Simple Blind Retrieve*

Blind retrieving is when the dog has no idea where the retrieve is. Everything we have done up until this point has been to enable the blind retrieve. It is a matter of confidence: the dog needs to establish in its head that when you send it out for a retrieve, in a specific direction, it will get to the retrieve. This is not a leap of faith – well, at the beginning it is – but a demonstration of trust in you and in its training.

Only when the simple retrieves above are working well should you introduce the blind retrieve. Again, this is best done on the woodland path or track, and immediately following a simple thrown retrieve. Do this first, and then release the dog to play. When it is off and away from you, surreptitiously drop the dummy in the middle of the path. Walk on twenty yards, recall the dog to your side, set it up exactly as you would for a seen retrieve, and send it to fetch – it may get the idea straight away, but you may need to help it on its way if it doesn't understand what you want. Do this by walking towards the retrieve, encouraging it to 'Go back', and eventually – even if you get right up to the dummy – it will retrieve it. Praise the dog immediately. Repeat the exercise the next day, and

*Setting the dog up for a blind retrieve at a field trial.*

persevere until the dog has the idea – but don't get angry with it, no matter *how* frustrating it may be, because the dog is uncertain and needs encouragement. Once this is working nicely, gradually increase the distance.

## Retrieving in a Given Direction

One of the keys to blind retrieving is the ability of the dog to run out in a straight line and in the direction indicated. We need to start indicating direction, and we do this by crouching down next to the dog with the arm outstretched in the direction desired. It is also important to have the dog's body aligned in the desired direction, with it sitting looking towards the point

of retrieve. It is useful now and again to move behind the dog and see where it is pointed – you may be surprised to find it's not in the direction you intended.

## Exercise: Line of Dummies

In this exercise, sit the dog, then walk out twenty-five yards with a dummy and drop it. Walk on a further twenty-five yards and drop another dummy – make sure the dog can see the drop, hold it up, bang it in your hands a couple of times to be sure that it's been seen, and drop it. Another twenty-five yards out, drop another one. Walk back and send the dog to retrieve all three, one after another. Before each retrieve, ensure that the dog is completely aligned in the direction required: move to its side, crouch down, stretch out your arm in the direction of the retrieve, and send it off. It is important to align the line of the dummies in a different direction every time so the dog gets the idea of starting on a line you indicate to it, rather than thinking it has to go towards a particular tree which has always been along the line of dummies that you set out, always in the same place and direction.

When this is satisfactory, extend the distance between the dummies, so that eventually the dog will be running a couple of hundred yards for the furthest retrieve. After a while, omit the first dummy so there are only two to retrieve, and then finally only set out the one dummy.

It is important to keep extending the distance, otherwise the dog may well become conditioned to go a certain distance for a retrieve and no further (as can happen with the dummy launcher). What we are aiming for is that the dog will keep running on a line until either it comes across the retrieve (or winds it) or you command it otherwise. Practically speaking, though, if the dog is able to go out over 250–300 yards, this is more than enough.

To build on the above, it is a simple matter to drop a dummy (so that the dog can see it) at the end of a field, or at the furthest point of a walk, sending the dog back for it at increasing distances every day. This can be alternated with dropping the dummy surreptitiously so the retrieve becomes a blind retrieve.

## Directional Control in the Blind Retrieve

The ability to direct your dog left, right and back, to stop it and to get it to come towards you, all at a distance, is a crucial part of field work. You should be able to direct your dog to go left, right, away from you and towards you in order to position it in the area of a retrieve. Before moving on to this phase, all the functions already covered should be in place, not necessarily perfect, but working most of the time.

## Simple Left/Right Split

Arm yourself with two dummies, or have a willing volunteer to act as dummy thrower for you. Ideally, you should do this exercise with the dog placed in front of a hedge, a wall or a fence so that it can only go left or right. Walk the dog to heel forwards ten yards, then turn round and sit the dog. Face the dog and move back a few steps. Throw one dummy out to the right to land about five yards away. Make sure the dog does not move. Then throw the other dummy the same distance in the other direction. If the dog is steady, back away slowly, still facing the dog so that you are in a better position to stop it going for one of the dummies before you tell it. Move back to the starting position, facing the dog, with one dummy out to its right and one to its left.

Now, with a puppy, it is always going to go and fetch the dummy that was thrown last, so this is the one you need to indicate it should retrieve (nominating which one it should retrieve comes later). Let us assume that the dummy out to your right was the last thrown. Move your right hand so that it is stretched upwards, palm forwards, then move the hand round in an arc out to the right, at the same time saying 'Out', and leaning the whole body to the right so as to make as big a movement to the right as you can. If all is well, the dog will go out in the direction indicated and fetch the dummy. As always, if it gets it right, big praise! Now send it for the other dummy from where you are.

Repeat the exercise, but this time the last dummy thrown should be on the opposite side, so the dog will first go the opposite way.

When this is working well, throw both dummies out left, or both out right. Now the dog has a choice of two. As the young dog will always go for the last dummy thrown, send it for this one first. Walk the dog to heel back to the starting point, and walk back to your mark. Now there is

one dummy out to one side of the dog. Send it for this one – remember to really exaggerate the signal, lunging your hand and body in the direction of the retrieve. You won't have to always make it so obvious: when the dog is proficient, a small gesture will have the desired effect. Remember that at long distances your signals will have to be seen, so big movements are needed.

One common fault is that you indicate to the dog to go right and it promptly goes left. This is simply that the previous work has not been properly consolidated, and often occurs when you are trying to increase the distance between you and the dog too quickly. Go back closer and consolidate again.

## Opposite Directions

Not all retrieves will be out to the left or right, and we will most likely be sending the dog from our side, so we need to be able to indicate any direction. To do this, we start by placing two dummies, one directly in front of the dog and one directly behind – that is, 180 degrees apart. Retrieve these one after the other. Then in addition to the two dummies front and behind, add two more dummies out to the left and right, so the four are at 90 degrees to each other: front and behind, left and right. Retrieve them in any order. Practise until the retrieving of the dummy indicated is perfect before moving on.

**Reduce the angle:** Fine-tuning this retrieve exercise is now a case of reducing the 90-degree angle, but it is important to do this progressively and slowly. You are striving to get the dog to retrieve, in the order you require, dummies that are placed at an angle of 45 degrees one to the next. This angle of difficulty is enough, and there is no need to try and reduce it further: once you have achieved this you will be able to retrieve anything successfully.

*OPPOSITE: Out! To the right: the exaggerated hand and body movement can be seen by the dog even from a distance.*

## Directional Exercises

Throw dummies to the right, left and behind the dog. When one has been retrieved, replace it with another one so that the dog always has the choice of three to go for. This way you can practise left, right and back. Occasionally send the dog in the same direction twice: they get used to being sent in a different direction each time, but rarely back to the same place – but beware, this is often encountered in working tests.

## *Wind Direction and the Blind Retrieve*

Before setting up your dog for a blind retrieve it is important to take the direction of the wind into account. In the diagram you can see that if the dog is sent on a line that would take it upwind of the dummy, it will not be able to scent it, and eventually, after hunting around for a while, it will stop and look at you for help (that's if you don't intervene and start to give it directions to the retrieve). It would be better if in the first instance you noted the direction of the wind, and sent the dog on a line where it would intersect the cone of scent being carried on the wind: so in this case, you would set up the dog to go off on a line to the left of the retrieve.

The length of the retrieve is also a consideration. Generally we expect the dog to run in a straight line in the direction we have indicated with our hand, and to keep going in that direction until either it comes across the retrieve or its scent, or until we intervene and command it to do something else. While this is true for other retriever breeds, it is only partially true for an HPR: the HPR will run as expected in a straight line in the direction indicated, but after a while it will start to turn, and will run more and more into the face of the wind until it is running directly into the wind. Quite when it starts to do this depends on the dog and how much space it perceives it has around it, but very roughly you can expect it to do so after 150 yards or so; however, it could be further, or a lot further, again

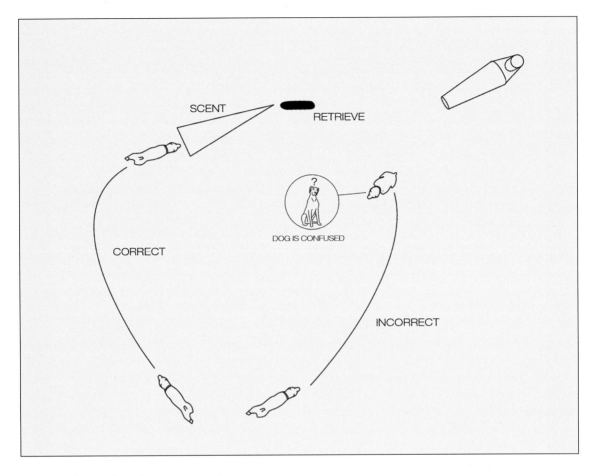

*Send your dog on a line where it can scent the retrieve.*

dependent upon that particular dog and the conditions prevailing at the time.

With this is mind, on a very long retrieve you would set the dog off on a line which, *if* it ran straight, would bring it to a position a long way downwind of the retrieve – but because of its natural tendency to curve into the wind, this will actually bring it into the cone of scent as depicted in the diagram. Experience will tell you how your own dog will behave, and so give you the intelligence to compensate. The training suggested in the 'Line of Dummies' exercise above (see page 78) will help to instil the idea of running directly back a long way, and will also extend the distance at which the dog will start to turn into the wind. (With a seen retrieve we would expect the dog to go straight to it, because it has been able to mark it, so there would be no need to set it up in this way.)

## Negotiating Obstacles in the Retrieve

A gundog may be called upon to make a retrieve that requires it to negotiate fences, gates and other obstacles. The command in this case is 'Over' or 'Get over'. Note that 'Over' may not necessarily mean an obstacle immediately in front of it, but that the dog is required to get over something that it will encounter at a distance. At a pond, 'Over' will mean 'swim to the other side' or to an island. If the dog is in front of a gate, 'Over' means jump the gate. In another situation, 'Get over' will send the dog 100 yards to a stile, which it then knows it has to jump in order to get to the retrieve – the dog will understand that the retrieve is not to be found before the obstacle, but that it has to 'get over' to find it. When out on the rough shoot, stiles and fences need to be climbed over or ditches crossed. Here, the command 'over' is used to indicate to the dog that it has to negotiate whatever obstacle is immediately in front of it. It's a lot for the dog to understand, but it will, given time and as it gains in experience.

A small stream (not deep, so that it can be waded) or a ditch (it doesn't matter if it is wet or dry) make good starter obstacles. Sit the dog just back from the edge of the obstacle and throw a dummy to the far side, then tell the dog to 'Get over!': as it is essentially a simple seen retrieve, and assuming the obstacle is not too daunting, this should be easily accomplished. Consolidate this a few times, then gradually move the start point further away from the obstacle; always use the 'Get over' command.

**The Jumping Lane**

A sheep pen and a jumping lane are useful training aids. It is unlikely that these are going to be available in your back garden, but a good training ground should have a jumping lane at least.

A jumping lane is simply a length of path with three or four gates placed along its length, each approximately 2ft 6in (65cm) in height, which is easily within the capability of any HPR. Do not, however, start your pup jumping until it is at least six months old, and then only over very low obstacles so that it hardly needs to jump: its bones will still be forming and will be relatively soft, they will not be able to stand the strain, and you run the very real risk of deforming the bones or causing fractures.

*Over! Country stiles are useful for training the dog to jump obstacles.*

*Young dog at the jumping lane.*

The first exercise is to walk the dog to the first hurdle, sit it, and then throw a dummy over the hurdle to land just on the other side. Walk the dog away a few yards, then send it with the command 'Get over', and as it approaches the hurdle shout 'Over!', making sure you do this *before* it reaches the hurdle: if it jumps over and makes the retrieve, all is well. Many dogs are confused by the obstacle, however, and may bounce around before it, motivated to get the retrieve but not sure how to get to it. If this happens, encourage the dog with further 'Over' or 'Get over' commands, which usually does the trick.

When this is consolidated, walk the dog to heel to the first hurdle, sit it, making it wait until you have got yourself over. Call 'Over!' to get the dog to jump over the hurdle, and then continue to walk with it to heel to the next one. Sit the dog and throw a dummy over this hurdle to land just on the other side. Walk back with the dog at heel, over the first hurdle (making the dog sit while you get over, as before) and back to your starting point. Send the dog off with the command 'Get over', and don't forget to shout 'Over!' just before the first hurdle, and 'Over!' just before the second. If the dog hesitates at any point, shout 'Get on'.

When this is all working well, move out to the furthest hurdle. Finally, position dummies half way between the intervening hurdles so the dog has multiple dummies to retrieve.

### The Water Retrieve

In the shooting field, at field trials and working tests, your dog will need to complete water retrieves, initially seen and later blind ones. It is best to get your pup used to water and swimming as early as possible, at about four months or so. You will need a puppy dummy to start with, and/or a small Kong, which is light and floats well. You may have a limited choice of water, but ideally you are looking for a very slow-running river or canal, or a pond or lake where there is a very shallow entry – meaning that the dog does not enter directly into deep water, but paddles in, with the lake or river bottom gently leading it into the deeper water where it can start to swim. You will also need your wellies on!

Furthermore, try to pick a day when it's warmer: this is not a problem during the summer months, when the dog is most likely very happy to get in and cool off, but in the depths of winter it might not be so keen. Although the water temperature will change very slowly in comparison to the air temperature, it does help if the air temperature is reasonably warm and dry – all HPRs have fairly waterproof coats, but cold air will still make things unpleasant for the young dog, and the last thing we want to do is put it off going in the water. Bring a towel

to rub it down. Don't attempt any swimming when there is ice, or if the water is near freezing – you will be asking for problems, and although these conditions can be handled easily by the older dog, don't try it with a pup.

Having an older dog with you is a good idea, to show the young dog what is going to happen; it is also useful in case it doesn't make the retrieve and you are left with the problem of fetching a dummy floating in the middle of a lake. So have the older one do a couple of retrieves with the pup watching. This may well have the effect of geeing up the pup so much that it can't wait to get in, and bounds in to fetch the dummy or Kong without any thought.

The young dog will demonstrate a whole range of reactions when it encounters water for the first time. If it bounds in without a care, count yourself lucky. More likely, it will treat the water with a certain amount of suspicion, and while it may be looking at the floating

*All HPRs are good swimmers.*

*Hungarian wirehaired Vizsla hunting hard.*

retrieve, it can't quite bring itself to brave the deeper water, and you'll need to help and encourage it: wade into the water yourself near to the edge, and encourage your dog to come with you – splash the water around with your hand and the dummy or Kong so that the dog joins in the game.

After a while, throw the dummy a very short distance – no more than a foot, or maybe two – where it is still in the shallows so the dog can easily fetch it by itself. Continue the game, but each time throw the dummy just a little further – as the water becomes deeper, throw the dummy less far, until eventually you can see that the dog has had to swim for it. Do this exercise once more, and then stop – but give a *lot* of praise. Keep doing this every few days, not every day, and you should have a confident water retriever.

## Retrieving to Hand

As with all other retrieves, the dog should deliver the retrieve to your hand. However, it is not necessary or even desirable to make the dog sit and present out of the water, so don't insist on it. When you start on water retrieves, make sure you stay close to the edge or bank so that you can take the dummy from the dog's mouth as soon as it is fully out of the water and on the bank. Don't pull the dummy out of its mouth, but be ready to take it at the earliest opportunity. Dogs often get into the habit of putting the dummy down as soon as they are out of the water to have a good shake before picking it up again. However, in tests they are not allowed to do this, and by keeping close to the edge you reduce the possibility of this happening. Your aim is to be able to move progressively back from the edge so you can send the dog, and it will be able to carry the dummy back to you over any distance without stopping on the way. If it starts to get into the habit of stopping, move right back to the water's edge again.

Later on, when the dog is able to respond to hand signals, it will be possible with some practice to control the dog while it is swimming.

## Hunting Training

While some dogs quarter naturally out of the box (off the lead and off they go, perfect wind management, quartering the ground beautifully with plenty of drive), others may need some help in establishing a good pattern. It helps to have an interesting ground, ground which is easy and inviting for the dog to run over, preferably with a hint of game scent or other interesting smells to perk it up. Open woodland is perfect, but cereal crops (as long as they are not too high), grass fields, stubble, sugar beet or other root crop and heather moorland are all eminently suitable.

In contrast to other whistle commands, the 'pip pip' of the 'turn' whistle is tightly aligned to the dog's hunting and quartering routine. For this reason we treat the 'turn' whistle as part of hunting training.

Usually the young dog will follow the direction that you, its owner or handler, are moving in – indeed, very young pups may not move far away from you at all, so wait until yours is starting to be more adventurous, either on its own or with another dog, before starting to teach the 'turn' whistle: too early and you could inhibit how far the dog is prepared to be away from you, particularly with those that need more encouragement to run out further from you. A hard-running dog, however, will need all the control you can exert to keep it from disappearing over the horizon, and with these the 'turn' whistle needs to be introduced very early on.

### The 'Seek On' Command

'Seek on' is the command used to start the dog off on its quartering pattern in search of game.

With the dog sitting by your side, take the slip lead off and put it in your pocket – you don't want it in the way at crucial moments, getting tangled up with it if it's around your neck, or in the way if you need to use hand signals.

Before setting the dog off – 'casting it off' – always check the direction of the wind and think how it will affect the dog's run: with a headwind, it doesn't matter too much which way you send the dog, out to the right or left. With the wind at an angle, send the dog away from you in the direction that is more downwind so that it has the longer length of run before it turns, naturally or on your whistle, into the wind. The young dog should always be run directly into wind, especially when you first start quartering. Indicate, by stretching out your hand, which way you want it to go, and say 'Seek on'. The young dog will usually take the command to mean 'Off you go then, and have a good run' (which it does, in the beginning), and off it goes. Later it will make the association between 'Seek on' and the joyful opportunity to go and find game, but for now we will be happy if it sets off with some purpose. Use 'Seek on' only when you want it to go and find game, and 'Off you go' or 'Go play' to release it for play.

'Seek on' is used not only to initiate quartering, but also to continue hunting when it has stopped, or been stopped. For example, a shot causes the dog to stop and sit, and you now have the following options: to recall it, send it for a retrieve, or tell it to resume hunting.

### Quartering

With the dog off the lead, cast it off as discussed previously with the 'Seek on' command and an indication as to the direction of the first cast. Wait until the dog has run out to one side of you, then turn and walk in the opposite direction with your back to the dog. Keep walking and wait for the dog to run by, at which point turn smartly again to walk off in the opposite direction. If the dog runs by but then stops and looks back, continue walking towards it, because this will have the effect of 'pushing' it further out. If it does start to run further, keep walking, because it may look back, but if it sees that you are still walking behind it in the same direction, it will keep going. If it does start to look back, speed up your pace and yell 'Go on, go on!' to encourage it to keep going. When it does, only then turn your back on it and move in the opposite direction again.

In doing this you are effectively walking a small version of the dog's quartering pattern, and you may find it is helpful to do this even when the dog is quartering nicely: you don't want to be walking the dog's beat for it, but it can encourage the dog just that little bit if it can see out of the corner of its eye that you appear to be walking in the same direction as it is going.

Hand signals can be used to indicate in which direction you want the dog to hunt, whether further to the right or left. The dog is very conscious of the set of your upper body, and it is possible to get the dog to change direction just by a slight movement of your upper body to the right or left.

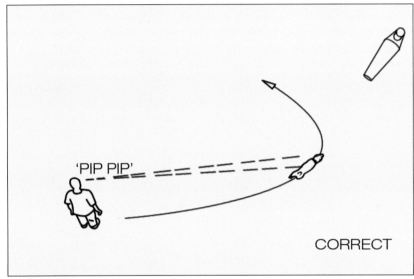

'PIP PIP'

CORRECT

*Teaching the 'turn' whistle. Be careful when you whistle.*

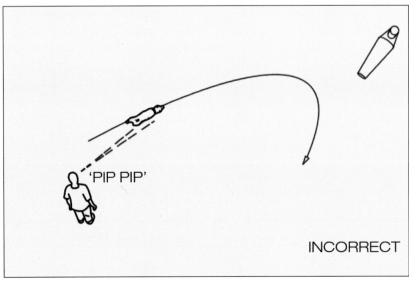

'PIP PIP'

INCORRECT

## The 'Turn' Whistle

The 'turn' whistle can be introduced much earlier, in the course of your daily walks. For example, a path branches off from the main path, and the dog goes off down it: wait until you've past the junction, but keeping an eye on the dog, which will run back towards you when finally it notices that you aren't behind any more. You need to catch this moment, and 'pip pip' your whistle *just as it is thinking about turning* to catch up with you. When it runs back to you, ignore it completely, and keep walking, because you don't want to establish the 'turn' whistle as the 'recall' whistle instead. Again, make sure that there is always a large distance between you and the dog before you use the 'turn' whistle.

The dog that quarters naturally still needs to be taught the 'turn' whistle, because this is the method by which the width of its beat is controlled. It will be necessary to do this for a variety of reasons: to keep your dog out of the way of other dogs in a beating line for example, or in a field trial where the judges have indicated the beat should be confined to between two outer guns or to one half of a field.

Teaching the free-running dog the turn signal requires a different technique: watch the dog carefully, and sound the 'pip pip' when you see that it is starting to turn upwind of its own accord, as it approaches the edge of a field for example. We also need to consider the timing of the 'turn' signal, and the position of the dog's ears in relation to your position: if it senses that the sound is greater in its left ear, it will turn towards that ear, and of course the same goes for the other ear, turning to the right. This may result in the dog turning in a direction that will take it downwind, rather than making a turn that takes it in an upwind direction.

Turning downwind is called 'Back casting' and is highly undesirable, principally because the dog is turning to run on a line that will take it over ground it has already covered – although some dogs can do it for unfathomable reasons, often when young; but it is not to be encouraged, and you must learn

not to encourage it by whistling it at the wrong time. In the diagram opposite, the handler is positioned back from the line of the dog's quartering pattern – as would be the case normally – but we can see that this is precisely the situation where the sound of the whistle will be perceived by the dog to be louder in its right ear, causing it to back cast, or turn downwind. So don't whistle, but wait until it starts to turn into the wind of its own accord, and then, and only then, whistle, certain that it is the *upwind* ear that hears your whistle. Run forwards to position yourself slightly ahead of the dog, and where you can safely whistle it so that it will turn into the wind.

If the dog, on reaching a hedge at the edge of the field, now starts hunting along the hedge line, get on the whistle to 'pip pip' it back towards you across the field. It is good that it's checking the hedge, but don't allow it to run up the hedge line too far, because it will be unwittingly taking a bigger bite than before as its turn has been disturbed, which may then cause it to miss ground or to 'bump' a bird.

You will probably get to see how this works while you are out with your dog, blowing the whistle with the dog turning the wrong way. Don't worry too much – it's not going to affect the dog if you get it wrong every now and again, but do learn from it when it happens.

All the foregoing may give the impression that much whistling is necessary, but this is definitely not the case – indeed, it is to be applauded if no whistle were employed at all. Everything so far has been centred round training, but once the correct response has been ingrained into our dog, then it is time to back off, and the less whistling there is, the better: try to be conscious of this, and only resort to the whistle almost as a last resort. As far as you can, do not disturb the dog's natural flow, but do help it if you think you can. The diligent hunting dog will be concentrating on its task, and it doesn't need a fly buzzing noisily and annoyingly round its head, disturbing its flow – your whistle. If you don't need to whistle, don't.

*Pointing grouse.*

## Pointing

The point is an instinctive reaction to scent, and a young dog may start its career by pointing the cat, butterflies, anything in fact. It will have its own instinctive list of things to point, instilled by selective breeding – but in the beginning it still has to make sense of what it is scenting. The moment will come when the scent of a game bird wafts into its nose and the reaction is usually startling: the dog has suddenly recognized a scent that its breeding tells it is definitely on the list of things to point, and so it does.

However, when the young dog starts to point, it must be told that it is doing the right thing.

Approach it slowly and from the side so it can see you in its peripheral vision – never approach a dog on point from directly behind, because in doing this you are sure to 'push' it forwards on to the bird, and may cause it to flush the bird before you are ready. Move slowly towards the dog blowing your whistle very gently, or saying 'Steady, steady' in soft, low tones. You should reach out and gently stroke the dog between the shoulders and along its back, saying 'Good boy, good dog' at the same time. Some trainers advocate getting down and cuddling it – anything to reassure it that it is doing exactly what you want it to. All this time the dog should remain absolutely still.

For the young dog a session or two in a rabbit pen, designed for the purpose, is an excellent way of encouraging the point and training it not to chase anything that moves, or to move anything, when it is on point.

## Introducing your Dog to Game

When the dog is retrieving dummies well, the introduction to game can be made, though quite how depends to a certain extent on the time of year. Probably the ideal time is during the shooting season when there is plenty of game available, but progress can be made out of season. The introduction to the smell and feel of dead game can be done very early on, even at a few months, but at this very early age it is a good idea not to allow the pup to mouth game as it tends to become too excited, and can bite into it overenthusiastically, whereas we want it to be careful in its handling of its retrieves. An ideal time to organize this introduction is at the end of the shooting day when all are gathered round the bag. With the pup on a lead, allow it to sniff around the birds, but keep it from actually grabbing them, even if it is tugging at the lead to get at them.

As a prelude to retrieving cold game, some trainers advocate the use of feather-covered dummies first, before moving on to the real thing – and certainly out of the shooting season; with the dog ready to progress, this is the only viable option (unless you happen to have some pheasant still languishing in the freezer). The sensible trainer saves some pheasant wings for this purpose. While scent will not be factor, it is important for the dog to become accustomed to the feel of the feathers in its mouth. During the shooting season cold game is readily available, and the options for the trainer are improved.

It is important to use freshly killed game that is undamaged. Young dogs may be put off by damaged game, and may well not wish to hold such birds at all. Start with pheasant or partridge – no woodcock or snipe at this stage. Either hold the bird in your hand, or lay it on the ground and let the dog sniff round it, allowing it to take the bird in its mouth if it wants to. Some will pick it up straight away, while others may take some time investigating this new thing, nuzzling around the feathers and trying to find the best way to pick it up. This is fine for the first or second time, and some encouragement may help, but don't allow the dog to start chewing the bird or playing around with it – take the bird away immediately if it starts to do this. Introduce the feathered dummy to the dog in the same fashion as real game, as has just been described above.

With the initial introduction over, try a simple retrieve. Any seen retrieve will do, but only a very short distance to start with, say ten yards or so. After sending the dog, if it picks it up straight away and comes back wagging its tail, this is a major milestone in its training programme. Make sure the bird is brought back to hand – though don't make a fuss about getting the dog to sit and present at this stage. (Some handlers never train their dogs to sit and present shot game, since in this case its job is to retrieve gently to hand, after all – nevertheless, a nice present does look good.)

Don't worry for the first few retrieves if the dog takes some time in picking the bird up: some dogs will pick up immediately, while others need some time to work out how best to pick it up – these may well start to come back with an obviously uncomfortable and awkward grip, but will put down the retrieve and re-adjust their hold. All this is perfectly acceptable in the beginning, but be alert for any sign of the dog just starting to play around with it, rather than making genuine attempts to find the best way of bringing it back to you. Any sign of play or messing around should be stopped with an 'Ah, ah!' or 'No!' And if the dog persists, run forwards, take the retrieve away, and start again.

# Chapter 7

# The HPR in the Field

We have described how the HPR hunts, points and retrieves, and in doing so, we are describing dogs bred to do this complete job of work for the game shot. It is its completeness, its ability to do all the tasks, which sets the HPR apart from any other breed of gundog. With our understanding of what it can do, and how it goes about doing it, we can now turn to how these skills can be used in the field.

## WORKING WITH THE DRIVEN SHOOT

The HPR is not ideally suited to the driven shoot, but there are very few shoots dedicated to the HPR dog, and many hundreds of driven or walk-and-stand shoots around the country — so if you wish to work your dog, the chances are that it will be on a driven-type shoot. Although

*One gun and his dog – all you need for a successful day in the shooting field.*

*A keeper who understands how HPRs work is invaluable.*

the driven shoot is not the natural home of the HPR, there are ways to make it useful to you as a training ground, and in the process become a useful member of the beating and picking-up team. We have seen earlier the scenario whereby an HPR on point can be disturbed by spaniels or other dogs working in the beating line, and how it is undesirable for the HPR to be worked in this way. Unfortunately, there will be times when it may be unavoidable: for example, if the beating team is short of dogs, when it would seem churlish for you to refuse the request to make up the line.

It is better to try and work at the extremities of the beat, out of the way of the other dogs in the middle of the line. There may be small woods or copses located off the main beating line that you could usefully work through, or hedgerows that lead up to a wood that will be beaten through, which you could run the dog down in the hope of pushing the birds into the wood. If your dog manages to find a bird to point and flush in the process, so much the better.

It is quite rare to have the luck to have a keeper, or whoever is in charge of the beaters,

who understands the HPR dog fully. Most will treat you and your dog with a certain amount of scepticism at the beginning, though they will rapidly come round to accept you both if you perform well – even if the HPR doesn't behave like the more common spaniel and labrador. It seems that many have the impression that the HPR is a pointer and not very good at retrieving, and if this is the impression they have, then no wonder that they will have little enthusiasm for such a dog on their shoot. After all, a dog that only points isn't very useful for the driven shoot, but if it won't retrieve either, then, well, it's no good to it at all.

This impression is outmoded and simply wrong: there may well be no smoke without fire, but this view dates from the times when there was no dedicated HPR training available, which meant the HPR dog was trained as a labrador or spaniel, with little or no regard given to its individuality. It is instructive to read books on rough shooting from the 1970s: these describe the most desirable attributes of a rough shooting dog – namely an ability to hunt, point and retrieve – and they discuss the relative merits of the labrador, spaniel, pointer and setter, with only passing reference to a pointer-retriever (as the HPR used to be termed) – and even then it was described with what can only be called some element of suspicion, a prejudice that lingers to this day.

Luckily, things have moved on from then. More recently, let's say in the last twenty to twenty-five years or so, the increasing use of the HPR in its own right has resulted in the development of highly effective, dedicated training, which has improved the HPR's overall performance beyond recognition. While it may be true that in any one dog its ability to hunt, point and retrieve may not be present in equal amounts – it may hunt and point well, but not be so good at retrieving – another dog may turn out to be a fantastic retriever, but not so good at game-finding: but this is all a question of degree. It is not that this particular dog cannot find game at all, but it's just not as good. Of course, the spaniels and labs present won't be perfect either, but they are already in the shoot and not under the same spotlight as you, with everything to prove. Let's lay this one myth to rest: the HPR can make a fantastic retriever.

One of the keys to this is to have an impeccably trained and well-behaved dog. Most of the spaniels or labradors on the shoot will be trained to a certain extent, but as far as the average beater is concerned, it doesn't matter if the dog 'runs in' on a retrieve (meaning that it runs to fetch the retrieve before it is commanded to do so) or if the game is chased. Present yourself to them with a dog that doesn't run wild in the beating line, can be held to a reasonable distance, is responsive to the whistle and which retrieves on command, and you will quickly be noticed, hastening your acceptance into the ranks of a regular at the shoot.

Be careful though, because if you present your dog as the ultimate machine that will single-handedly sweep through forty acres of wood, finding all the game in it and retrieving everything shot, you will be very unpopular

with the other beaters who value the contribution made by their dogs – and rightly so. The HPR has a place on the shoot, its own niche, but the spaniel and lab are 'the Establishment' and they do all that is asked of them, being bred and trained to perform the tasks of the driven shoot. Your job is to find your own place working beside the existing team of beaters and pickers-up.

Of course, it may well not be possible to arrive with the finished article, and you may well be hoping the shoot can be a training ground for your dog. This is not going to work. You can certainly improve on your dog's performance, particularly at retrieving, by working on the shoot, but it is not going to be a substitute for dedicated training.

We saw earlier that the HPR does not mix well with the spaniels in a beating line because they will flush everything they find, while we want the HPR to point the birds. So in general, try to avoid being put in the line of beaters and spaniels, but if it's unavoidable, keep the dog on the lead. Long beating lines with few dogs far apart may leave sufficient room between dogs for the HPR to range a meaningful beat. This situation occurs when there aren't as many beating dogs as usual, so the amount of ground covered by each available dog has suddenly increased. For the HPR, this is the perfect chance to show what it can do – ranging out on either side, covering a large area which the other breeds cannot possibly cover, while moving the line forwards at a reasonable pace. Even if the HPR has a staunch point which requires the handler to close in to initiate the flush, it is likely that the find will be in front of the other dogs that tend not to range out so far in front as the HPR, and so little, if no time is lost.

Try, if possible, to agree with whoever is in charge of the beaters to work the ends of the beating line and along hedgerows. Quite often there will be hedgerows they will be happy for you to work down if you ask them – especially if they don't have many dogs for the beating line and wouldn't be sending them off to do the hedgerows anyway: the hedges that start a long way out from the main drive, but which lead down to it, are a good example, because running the dog along them can stop birds from running away from the main drive, pushing them back instead.

After a time, those on the shoot – particularly the important ones such as the shoot captain and the keeper – may show an interest in your HPR and recognize its value. It is a sign of this acceptance when you are asked 'You've a wide-running dog, just work the top end of the wood through, would you?' Be patient and it will happen to you.

## PICKING UP

The job of the picking-up dogs is, as the name suggests, to find and retrieve game that has fallen. Many of the guns will have their own dogs on the peg beside them, but many won't, so these positions need to be covered. The gun, however, has to concentrate on reloading and shooting, and has no time to pay attention to his dog. Once sent, the gun cannot devote any time to handling the dog on to a retrieve, and will therefore leave birds that have fallen further away and which the dog may have difficulty finding without some help from a handler. This is where the picking-up dog comes in. For you and your HPR, picking up does have some training merit because the dog gets to retrieve, it can also help with steadiness, and some retrieves can be challenging enough to make it a thoroughly good training day. If you have a busy day the dog will have an enjoyable day out.

## THE ROUGH SHOOT

The rough shoot is the perfect place for the HPR, and is where it really comes into its own. A few invited shooting friends, and a few HPR dogs that are run singly in turn, is a highly effective and

*Picking up is an enjoyable day out.*

enjoyable way to spend a day shooting, with no beaters or flags necessary. This is the best scenario for you to work your dog, and the best situation for it to be trained. Unfortunately there are very few opportunities to work in this way, but they do exist: your local HPR club may be able to help, and if you become a regular at one of the local driven shoots, it may be possible to persuade them to have a walked-up day, or even let you take your dog out on your own. In the latter case it is better for you to concentrate on handling your dog and have someone else come along with a gun. Two guns are perfect. Don't be tempted to take the dog out with your gun unless you are absolutely confident that it is steady to flush and to shot – you can't be shooting and handling the dog at critical moments: you must know that it will behave correctly. Many highly experienced handlers who are excellent shots will elect either to run their dog or to shoot, but not both, and it is an excellent arrangement to have the possibility to do both during the course of the day by swopping dog for gun.

## THE HPR IN FALCONRY

The HPR is finding a perhaps surprising acceptance as part of the falconer's team. It is a type of hunting with an enthusiastic and expert following: it represents a fascinating sport in its own right, and the relatively recent introduction of the HPR dog significantly extends the compass of the hunter with the falcon. It is also an ancient sport, formerly one of kings and the aristocracy, and has been practised in the UK for well over 450 years. 'Falconry' is the umbrella term for those who fly falcons; those flying hawks are more correctly termed 'Austringers'. Beginners to the sport usually train with a Harris hawk or a red-tailed hawk, both of which can operate over a variety of terrain and can take a range of quarry; other more specialized breeds are only suitable for certain types of countryside. The peregrine falcon, goshawk and merlin are suited to the experienced handler, being generally harder to train.

The basic attributes for a dog to be of use with this ancient art must be hunting drive and the ability to cover large areas of ground, it must point game, be steady to the flush, and able to work at a distance from the handler while staying in contact so control can still be maintained. The HPR is well suited to this type of work, and many of the breeds are actively working today: the Brittany, the German short-haired pointer, the German wire-haired pointer, the Hungarian Vizsla and the Hungarian wire-haired Vizsla being the most prominent.

The HPR is sent off to quarter the ground in search of game, coming on point when it has located suitable quarry, and having to remain on point possibly for some considerable time while the handler releases the hawk into the air. When the bird has gained sufficient height, the handler can signal the dog to flush the bird into the air: the flushed bird is easily spotted by the hawk (which has learned that the dog is the thing to keep its eye on), which dives with tremendous speed – up to 200mph (320km/h) – taking the flying bird from the air. If the hawk misses, the dog is commanded to hunt on.

Using the dog in this way allows a tremendous amount of ground to be covered, and the three protagonists in this play all learn the usefulness of the other. The training to reach the standard required of both dog and hawk is very lengthy, requiring time and commitment to both, a commitment that can only be given by a few very dedicated to the sport – it is definitely not something you can expect to pick up quickly, and the keeping of a bird of prey is a very specialized business.

# Chapter 8

# Working Tests

Working tests for HPR breeds are held between March and September and are a great way of training your dog out of the shooting season, as well as being a thoroughly enjoyable day out amongst friends. Tests are set which simulate tasks a dog would be expected to perform on the shooting field, canvas training dummies being used in place of game (although cold game may occasionally be encountered in the Open classes); each test is scored by a judge, and at the end of the day, awards are presented to the best performing dogs.

Working tests are very popular and well attended events; they are run by the various breed and HPR gundog societies, with entries drawn from those who work their dogs on shoots or participate in field trials, but equally from those who enjoy the working tests as an end in themselves, and for whom the event provides a good day out with their dog. Some of the events are staged at spectacular locations: country estates or stately homes, to which one would not normally have the privilege of access, and this really enhances the sense of a 'day out'.

*The working test is a great day out with your dog.*

There are different classes of entry, broadly reflecting the experience and age of the dog, namely Puppy, Novice and Open (the definitions appear later). Working tests are run under Kennel Club rules, with only the Puppy, Novice and Open classes recognized by the KC. Some societies have a Graduate class as a stepping stone for those who have qualified to compete in the Open classes, recognizing the fact that competing in Opens requires a much greater level of ability and control than would be encountered in Novice, and which the newly qualified Open dog may not yet possess. Special Beginners classes are also occasionally available, designed for those who have not yet competed in a working test. These are invaluable as introductory sessions, and are always well subscribed.

There are no limits to the number of entries in any one class; an average class entry would be about ten in Puppy, thirty-five in Novice and twenty in Open, with some events attracting entries of well over 100 dogs.

## AM I READY?

Those thinking about entering a working test for the first time are often worried whether they, or their dog, have the necessary skills to take part. The best way to find out is to go along to a working test as an observer, see the classes in action, and take the opportunity to talk to the competitors who will be delighted to help answer the many questions you probably have. Later on in this chapter you will find some of the tests described: study these to see if you think they could be attempted by you and your dog – but if not, don't worry, because some working tests include a Special Beginners class, designed for those who are contemplating entering a test for the first time, or for those who are interested in the working abilities of their dog but don't know how to get started. These classes are taken by experienced HPR trainers

who will put you at ease and help you towards the goal of competing, or will help you if you decide you want to put more effort into the training of your gundog. The most important thing is to make the first step.

If, on the other hand, you think that you are capable of tackling some of the tests, then by all means have a go and enter.

## ENTERING A WORKING TEST

You will need to fill in an entry form which you can obtain from the working test secretary or co-ordinator, or you can download it from the web site of the society promoting the event. Note that as working tests are held under Kennel Club rules, the entry form is of an approved type and so must be used and completed in full. Unlike a field trial, there is no limit imposed on the number of dogs in a class (although some societies do have class size limits of their own, so check the schedule carefully), so you can be assured of taking part unless some catastrophic event occurs and the event is cancelled. You will not receive any confirmation of your entry, but assuming the post has done its job, you will be entered and expected to appear. It is possible to enter on the day, but this is entirely at the discretion of the working test committee, and with the more popular events it is unlikely to be allowed. Always, therefore, enter by post well in advance of the event.

### Classes to Enter

Every working test has Puppy, Novice and Open classes, but some may have Special Beginners, Graduate or Yearling classes, any or all of them at the discretion of the society. Check the schedule carefully to find out which classes you are eligible for. You may enter more than one class, and indeed many do, entering both Puppy and Novice when the younger dog is getting to the age limit of the Puppy class and will have to compete in Novice very soon anyway. The classes are defined as follows:

**Puppy:** Confined to dogs over six months and not older than eighteen months of age on the day of the test.

**Novice:** Confined to dogs that have not gained an award or Certificate of Merit at a field trial, have not been placed first, second or third in an Open working test, or first in a Novice working test.

**Open:** Open to all dogs of a specified breed or breeds, although preference may be given to dogs that have gained an award or Certificate of Merit in a field trial, have been placed first, second or third in an Open working test, or have won a Novice working test.

## COMPETITION DAY

### *What to Take*

- Two canvas dummies for the dog, clearly marked with your name in waterproof ink. The 1lb ones are used – don't take the much smaller puppy dummies.
- There will be a break for lunch usually at around midday and lasting an hour or so. This is a welcome break for all, especially for the judges, stewards and dummy throwers who will have been working non-stop. Some events do have food available, which is advertised on the schedule if this is the case, but usually you will need to make your own arrangements for a picnic lunch.
- Money for the raffle: most of the societies have a raffle, for which tickets are sold at lunch time, with the draw taking place at the end of the day, usually just prior to the awards ceremony. The proceeds go to the society, usually with a proportion going to charity or to the society's rescue scheme.

- Water for the dogs: it may well be a hot day, so make sure you have water available for your dogs to drink at all times. Do not rely on water being available on the ground; even though there will be a water test, it may be located some way away from the parking area.

On arrival, check in at the reception tent where your entry and class(es) will be confirmed. You will receive a sticker with your number and class, along with a printed programme that will list the running order for that class.

The chief steward will call everyone together to make the initial announcements, to introduce the judges and stewards, and point out the location of the various test areas, as well as other 'housekeeping' notices. This done, it is up to you to find your way to the first test.

### *Class Stewards*

The steward manages the list of those scheduled to run in the class, and is the liaison between the judge and competitors, the judge relying on the steward to have the next dog ready to run when required. Report to your class steward as soon as you arrive, and they will check you off on their list of runners. Once you are there, do not leave without first telling the steward: it is a courtesy, and will spare them the hassle of trying to find you if you are next to run.

Dogs are run in the numerical order published in the programme, but it is not obligatory to do so, and there are usually departures to the published order for a variety of reasons. First and foremost, it is usual for those who are running in more than one class to be given priority, and for these competitors to run as soon as possible so they can then go off immediately and complete tests in their other class. At some events, the stewards' list will already indicate those who have multiple entries, but check with them anyway, and when initially reporting to the steward, tell them you if are running in another class.

It is important to realize that it is not a right to take your run in front of others, but a courtesy afforded to you by the steward and your fellow competitors. It does not go down well if you bounce up and brightly demand that you run next and in front of others, who may well have been waiting some considerable time for their turn. Be considerate, tell the steward (if you have not already done so) that you are in another class, and then leave it up to them to fit you into the running order.

## THE TESTS

There are usually four separate tests that need to be completed: hunting/quartering, seen retrieve, blind retrieve (not puppy), and water. In most working tests, hunting is marked out of forty, and the remaining three tests are each marked out of twenty, to give a maximum of 100 points; however, an equal twenty-five points for each test may also be used.

Each class has a steward and judge, and one or more helpers to throw dummies or fire a dummy launcher. The steward is responsible for the smooth running of the class by making sure the competitors are ready to go forwards to start their tests when the judge signals for the next dog, checking that those who arrive are on the list and in the correct class, as well as performing the necessary juggling acts with those who are booked in to more than one class.

Tests are set by the working test secretary in consultation with the judges. Ideally, the tests should be set such that they are well within the expected ability level of the class. If the tests are too easy, they are really no test, but if, on the other hand, they are too difficult and only a minority of the dogs are able to complete them, then the test fails as a method of enabling a comparison of relative ability. The test is at the right level when every dog is able to complete it. The judge then has the task of scoring how well the test was completed by each dog,

resulting in a much more satisfactory comparison of the working abilities of those on the day, which is the whole point of the working test. Some working test secretaries do seem to delight in conjuring up the most devilishly difficult tests in order ' to sort them out', which to my mind is completely the wrong thing to do – the tests are not there to eliminate all but the most capable (or just lucky) dogs, but to reveal the comparative abilities of *all* the dogs.

'Next dog!' is the universal signal for the next dog to come up to the judge to do its test. Make sure you give your number to the judge so that your mark goes in the right place. Dogs are usually run in numerical order, but not always, and the judge cannot assume that as No. 9 has just run, the next dog will be No. 10; so do give your number when you are called up.

The judge will explain to each handler the nature of the test in detail, what will happen (for example, a dummy will be thrown), and what is expected of the handler and the dog to complete the test satisfactorily. Listen carefully, and do ask if something is not clear. Make sure that you understand exactly what the test consists of, and how it is to be done, and ask again if you are not sure. Most tests require you to follow a certain sequence, and this must be done to the letter: points will be deducted or a zero score recorded if the required sequence is not followed.

When all is clear and you are happy to proceed, remove the lead, put it in your pocket out of the way, and send your dog.

Typical tests you will encounter are described below. This is by no means an exhaustive list, but it does cover most of those to be found. This is useful not only for the beginner, who will want to know what to expect, but also for those who are moving up to the next level and have no idea what to expect.

### Hunting – All Classes

The hunting (or quartering) test is for all classes, and is designed to assess the dog's ability to quarter the ground in search of game, as it would be expected to do in the shooting field. In all the classes there will be a piece of ground that the dog will be expected to quarter, so the judges can assess its performance. The size and quality of the ground varies widely according to the venue, each class usually having its own allotted piece of ground. The length of time a dog may be expected to run is dependent upon the size of ground available, but assuming there is unlimited ground, then an assessment over a reasonable length of time will be made by the judge, taking into consideration the number in the class and the prevailing weather conditions: if there are thirty dogs in the class (not unreasonable for Novice) and the judge elects to run each dog for ten minutes, this equates to five hours' total time, which will not leave enough time to complete any of the other tests. If the day is very hot and sunny it would be unreasonable to run any dog for too long. Adjustments are therefore made on the day.

In Puppy classes the handler may well be expected, at a signal from the judge, to blow his whistle for the dog to stop and sit wherever it happens to be, and then recall the dog again using the whistle only when directed by the judge. Another favourite, and one which is becoming more prevalent, is to recall the dog from where it is sitting, and while it is on the way back to you, to blow the 'stop' whistle again and get it to sit about halfway back to you before recalling it again to come all the way back.

Novice and Open dogs can expect distractions such as a dummy fired from a launcher to test steadiness to shot. The dog will be expected to sit or at least stop to the shot, and mark the fall of the dummy, which may, or may not, subsequently be retrieved. Variations on this are that the dog is sent for the retrieve from where it is sitting, or the dog is recalled to you first and then sent. Alternatively, you may be asked to hunt on to the end and send the dog back for the retrieve then.

A favourite in Open classes is for the handler to throw a dummy out to the left or right at the very start of the test, but the dog is not to retrieve it, but must hunt on up the ground, only being sent back for the retrieve right at the end. In addition, the judge may ask the handler to sit the dog (with the whistle) at any point (but usually towards the end of the run), and then ask for the dog to be sent back for the retrieve from where it is sitting. As it is much easier to send the dog back for a retrieve when you are next to it and able to direct it, ask the judge whether you can go to the dog to send it. You may be refused but it's worth asking. This has a better chance of being granted if you are the first dog to run, but the judge then has to grant the request to each subsequent dog.

## Retrieving Tests

Retrieving plays a big part in the working test, and for many this presents a great training opportunity: you are away from your home ground so the situation is new to the dog, and the design of the retrieve is not in your hands so you will not have any idea of the retrieve you are about to face – and nor does the dog! At home, on familiar ground, it can be difficult to come up with different retrieve scenarios, and dogs get to know the variations on a theme and are able to carry them out easily. It is useful to put them in unfamiliar surroundings, which will really put their training to the test: it is interesting to see how they perform, any shortcomings or failures providing you with a list of things that need to be worked on back home.

When you start out on working tests, this list might seem dauntingly long, especially in the move from Novice to Open tests, but persevere and value the learning experience. One of my dogs won a field trial award while still eligible for Puppy classes in working tests, which meant having to compete at Open level the following summer, so we spent the whole working test season coming nowhere in the Open rankings, but learning all the time. The following season

*Memory retrieve.*

we managed a first in an Open class, along with a succession of higher placings throughout that and subsequent seasons.

### Puppy Retrieving Tests

The tests in the Puppy class must take into account the ability of a dog at six months (the minimum age), although dogs up to eighteen months of age can compete in the same class. Quite clearly, a dog of nearly eighteen months will have a much greater ability than the very young dog, and may well be competing in Novice tests already; nevertheless the tests must be set so they are within the ability range of the youngest. All the retrieves are seen – the dog is able to see the throw, and mark where the dummy falls – and so the four tests will be hunting, first seen retrieve,

second seen retrieve, water. Here is a selection of tests that you might encounter:

**Memory Retrieve:** Walk the dog to heel for approximately thirty yards (or to a marker). Sit the dog and throw the dummy forwards a short distance. Walk back to the start with the dog at heel. On command from the judge, send the dog for the dummy.

**Half-Way Back:** Walk the dog at heel approximately thirty yards to the furthest marker. Sit the dog. Throw the dummy a short distance in front of the dog. Walk back to the middle marker with the dog at heel. Sit and leave the dog. The handler then walks back to the start and sends the dog back for the dummy.

*Half-way back.*

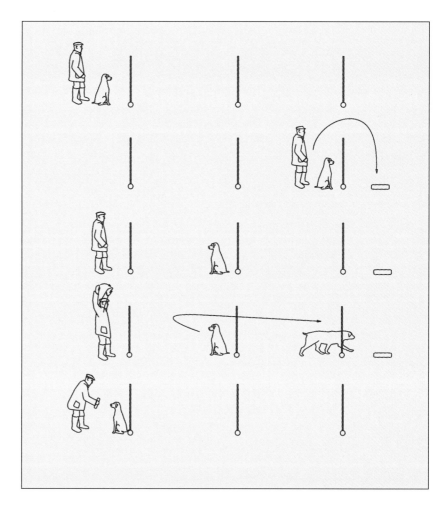

**Half-Way Back with Recall:** This is a variation of the previous test, the difference being that instead of sending the dog back for the retrieve, you recall the dog – whistle your dog to come to you – and then send it for the retrieve. This is a good exercise because the dog is expecting to go and get the retrieve straight away, as this is what your training has told it to do. Here we are exerting that little bit more control, and it is a good lesson for the dog to learn: not to anticipate the next command, but to watch and listen for it.

**'L' Retrieve:** This is another variation on the half-way back test. Walk from the start to a stake, turn right (or left) and continue to another stake. You leave the dog sitting at the stake where you

turned, and either send it for the retrieve from there, or recall it first and then send it.

**Seen Retrieve:** Sit your dog at the start with the lead off. Signal to the judge that you are ready. He will in turn signal to the dummy thrower, who will make a noise to attract the dog's attention and then throw the dummy. The judge will tell you to 'send your dog' for the retrieve.

**Simple Split:** Walk the dog forwards to the mark, and sit it. Throw one dummy out to the right of the dog, and one out to the left. Walk the dog back to the start. Send the dog for the first dummy (it doesn't matter which one in this test), and then for the other.

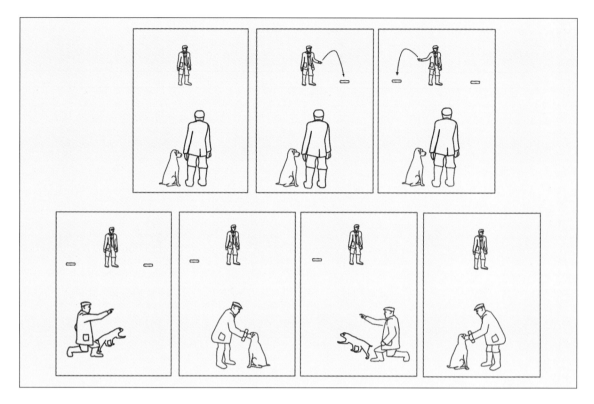

*ABOVE: Split retrieve.*

*BELOW: Dogs must be able to retrieve from water.*

**Water:** The water retrieve will be a dummy thrown a short distance from the edge of the water. The entry for the dog will be chosen so that it is shallow and gently sloping to make it as easy for the dog to enter the water as is practical at the site available.

### Novice Retrieving Tests

In the Novice class, both seen and blind retrieving is expected. A blind retrieve is when the dog has no idea where the dummy is. In this case the judge will indicate to the handler where the dummy is, or the area in which the dog should look. The Novice dog will be expected to perform quite complex tasks, should be able to do all the gundog tasks, and should be controllable from a distance.

**Seen Retrieve:** A dummy is thrown to land about 100 yards away. There will be some kind of sound made to attract the attention of the dog, a loud whoop or a shot from a starting pistol. The person throwing the dummy may not be in view, so it is important that the dog catches sight of the dummy in the air. Often the thrower is hidden behind a hedge or at the edge of woodland. Ask the judge where the dummy will be thrown from (if it's not obvious) and set your dog up to be looking in the right direction before telling the judge you are ready. If the dog doesn't see the flight of the dummy and is unable to mark the point of fall, then the test has suddenly transformed into a much harder blind retrieve. Use of the command 'Mark' or 'Watch' may help to gain the attention of the dog, which is all to the good, because it is amazing the number of dogs that just happen to look away at the critical moment when the dummy is in the air!

Sometimes a dummy launcher is used for the seen retrieve, and the 'bang' it makes will make any dog sit up and pay attention. Sometimes it is very difficult to see the dummy in flight, particularly if the launcher has been angled to get the best distance – the dummy is then thrown high into the air where it may be almost invisible to both dog and handler.

**Blind Retrieve:** As the name suggests, a blind retrieve is when the dog has no sight of the dummy and no idea where it has fallen. The judge will give the handler a 'Mark' – that is, he will point out the area where the dummy is to be found. Note the use of the word 'area': the job of the handler is to direct the dog into the general area where the retrieve is to be found, and to keep the dog in that area (usually by the use of the 'Hi lost' command), leaving it to hunt around until it can scent the dummy. Here it is most important for the handler to consider the direction of the wind, and to send the dog on a line that will position it downwind of the area of retrieve and so enhance the chance of it finding it quickly. If the dog arrives upwind of the retrieve it will be much harder work to signal it into a downwind position.

**Split Retrieve:** The dummy thrower will stand about thirty yards in front and throw one dummy out to the left and another out to the right, attracting the attention of the dog before each throw either by hand claps or by making a whooping noise. The judge will nominate which dummy is to be retrieved first, and this is the big difference from the puppy split, where it doesn't matter which one is picked first. In this test, marks will be deducted if the dog retrieves the wrong dummy.

**Split Retrieve with Dummy Launcher:** As above, but a dummy launcher is used to hurl a dummy. The bang, the flight and the bounce and roll of the dummy from the launcher makes a much more tempting retrieve, with the dog all keyed up ready to go. So, quite often, the test will be to leave the dummy from the launcher and retrieve the second, thrown dummy first.

**Seen into a Sheep Pen:** The dummy thrower will make a whooping noise to attract the dog's

*The sheep pen.*

attention, then throw the dummy into the middle of the pen. The dog is sent to retrieve it, but only when the judge tells you to send the dog. Rarely encountered (but a regular feature at one society), this test always catches many dogs out, as it is not often practised by many handlers, so try to find a pen or similar enclosure where you can practise.

**Open Retrieving Tests**

Open dogs are expected to be able to make long, blind retrieves over obstacles (including water) and over distances of 100 yards or even more. The tests are similar in design to the ones encountered in Novice, but the distances are much greater and the blind retrieves much longer, and, with the dog often out of the handler's sight, can be very challenging indeed. Most handlers new to the Open class, having won a Novice working test, are surprised at

the jump in difficulty, and for this reason some working tests have a Graduate class as a stepping stone. As success in retrieving is important in building confidence in the dog, take the opportunity and enter Graduate classes if they are available.

**Long Blind:** A retrieve over a very long distance (over 100 yards), with the dog often out of sight of the handler. The judge will give you a 'Mark', after that, send your dog...and hope.

**Blind into Sheep Pen:** A single dummy is thrown into a sheep pen about 100–150 yards away. This test is not often encountered, but is a regular feature at two working tests every year, and always causes problems for many dogs.

**Blind Retrieve over a Hidden Obstacle:** A dummy is placed on the far side of an obstacle such as a low gate or stile (something the dog can be expected to negotiate), which is out of sight of the dog and handler: for example, the stile is 100 yards down a path in the middle of a wood, the path having a bend in it.

**Double Blind into a Wood:** Two dummies are placed in a wood not far from each other, say five or ten feet. The difficulty here is that the dog is used to being sent in completely different directions for retrieves, as in the split retrieves, and it is rarely sent back out for the next retrieve on exactly the same line as the first, which often causes confusion.

**Seen Dummy Launcher with Bolting Rabbit:** The dummy launcher is fired and the dog sent for the retrieve. On the way back a bolting rabbit is released across its path as a distraction, and should be ignored by the dog.

**Blind and Dummy Launcher:** The dummy is fired from the launcher first with the dog (hopefully) marking the fall. The dog should leave this and be sent to retrieve another dummy first, usually in a completely different direction. The judge will give the handler a mark on the area of the blind retrieve. On retrieving this, the dog is then sent for the dummy from the launcher.

**Seen Water Retrieve:** The dummy thrower will be hidden from sight at the other side of a lake and fires a starting pistol to attract the dog's attention, quickly followed by the dummy thrown up into the air for the dog to see.

**Blind Water Retrieve:** Long, blind water retrieves are a real challenge and are usually planned to be the only test taking place towards the end of the day so that everyone can watch. The swims are usually 100 yards or so.

**Islands:** Sometimes the blind or seen retrieve will involve an island, with the retrieve somewhere on the island. A more difficult variant encountered occasionally is when the island is the half-way point to the retrieve, requiring the dog to get out of the water, up on to the island, then to re-enter the water on the far side, and swim out to the bank where the retrieve is to be found.

**Rivers/Streams:** In this test, as encountered at one notable venue, the dog is required to cross one stream or small river, and on reaching the far bank is required to cross another to find the retrieve on the furthest bank.

## JUDGING THE TESTS

In judging the tests, the judge has the difficult task of assessing how each individual dog has performed the task at hand. The assessment is of the dog, not the handler, but note will be taken of the performance of the team. This is more the case when the handler has to be involved in the success of the task, for example, with a blind retrieve where some handling of the dog may be necessary.

### Hunting

The judge is looking for drive, how enthusiastically the dog sets about its task, ground treatment and control. It should exhibit a good quartering pattern, having regard for the prevailing wind. It should cover its ground thoroughly, and be attentive to the handler, reacting to both whistle and other commands promptly. Each breed of dog has its own style of hunting, and the judge will use his knowledge of the different breeds to assess the dog on its own merits. Thus the slower trotting Italian Spinone will not be at a disadvantage against the faster German shorthaired pointer if both do their job well.

With working tests held in the summer months, it is quite often very hot on the day, which can affect the performance of the dog – some are more afflicted by heat than others. The

*A German shorthaired pointer making a clean pick-up.*

judge will already have adjusted the length of the test to suit the weather conditions, so that a dog will not be expected to run for too long when it is hot. This will inevitably have some impact on the validity of the test to assess hunting ability if the time allotted for the test is short. This is merciful at least to the dog, because the last thing it wants on a blazing hot day is to have to go off running in the open sun, when what it *really* wants is to hide in the shade under the nearest tree.

### Retrieving

With all retrieving the outrun should be with enthusiasm, in a straight line, with the pick-up clean and the retrieve delivered back to hand. The judge will take a dim view of dogs that relieve themselves at any stage of the retrieve, particularly on the way back; on the outrun

there may be a case for leniency because the dog may well have been standing or sitting for some time on the lead before coming up to do the test. On the return, however, the dog is merely being naughty.

A clean pick-up is where the dog arrives at the dummy, gathers it into its mouth quickly, and starts off immediately on its way back. Some dogs scarcely seem to stop, scooping up the retrieve while on the run and turning quickly to come back. The dog that stands over the retrieve looking at it, or which messes about nuzzling it or playing with it, will be marked down. Marks may also be lost if the dummy is dropped and has to be picked up again.

The delivery to hand should be just that: the dog nears the handler, slows down, but comes right up, offering the retrieve to the handler, who should only have to bend down slightly to remove the dummy, with the dog releasing its grip at the same time. This 'present' does not have to be with the dog sitting down: it may look very nice, and many handlers put a lot of training effort into this final phase, but this is unnecessary as it will not gain you any extra marks – the job of the dog is to deliver to hand, whether sitting or not, and as long as it does this well, either method is perfectly acceptable. The working tests are designed to show the working abilities of the dog as it would be expected to work in the shooting field, and there, the handler is only interested in the bird being delivered to hand without any other pretensions. What will lose you marks is a flying rugby tackle on the dog as it thunders past you towards the spectators, or the dog that takes a couple of circuits around you playing to the gallery, or which does a perfect present – but to your behind.

The judge will note how you have set up the dog for the retrieve, particularly in regard to the wind, and although this is not a consideration for the marking, your approach to the way the retrieve is to be done may well decide the outcome, and hence the mark recorded for the whole exercise. For example, if the dog is set off on a line that will bring it upwind of the retrieve so that it then has to be handled by whistle and hand signal, this would result in a lower mark than the handler that sets the dog up to run on a line that brings it into the vicinity of the retrieve, but downwind of it, such that the dog can scent it and bring it back without any input from the handler. The higher mark given would be because of the more efficient retrieve; marks would have been deducted for the whistling and hand signalling in the other situation, the overall retrieve in this case being less efficient. Marks will not have been

*A fast return will gain credit*

deducted because the judge saw that the dog was not being set up correctly, and was therefore always going to be at a disadvantage, but he may well have something to say to the handler at the conclusion of the test, given as friendly advice.

### Seen Retrieve

A seen retrieve should consist of a single command to set the dog off on its way, and the dog should run out quickly, with enthusiasm, in a straight line, picking up the retrieve without any fuss, returning quickly and delivering to hand. Any deviation from this will result in marks being deducted.

### Blind Retrieve

By their very nature, blind retrieves will almost always mean some element of handling to steer the dog into the vicinity of the retrieve. The judge will therefore not deduct marks for a reasonable amount of handling – though quite what 'reasonable' is, remains entirely the province of the judge. But clearly, a dog that makes a good retrieve with the minimum of handling is going to achieve a higher mark.

### Steadiness

Steadiness to shot or to fall is of utmost importance in the shooting field, and is treated with equal importance in the working test. The dog must remain steady – that is, it stops, and ideally sits – when it hears a report (at a working test from a dummy launcher or starting pistol) and/or when it sees a dummy in flight and falling. It should mark the point of fall, and only set off to retrieve when commanded to do so. In tests requiring steadiness, a zero mark will be recorded if the dog 'runs in' – the judges will give some latitude to Puppy and Novice dogs, and may only deduct a few marks if the dog can be stopped by the handler within a reasonable distance, but Open dogs will be expected to be totally steady.

### Water Retrieve

The key things the judge is looking for in the water retrieve is a clean entry with no hesitation, swimming in a straight line, making a clean pick-up, and a direct return journey. A dog that runs up and down the bank in an effort to find what it thinks is a more suitable entry point will have marks deducted: this is a common fault with many, exhibiting a lack of confidence usually stemming from a lack of practice, or lots of practice at the same pond, using the same entry. The entry for the water retrieve will be chosen to accord with the level of the dog: Puppy classes will have a very gentle sloping entry; the Novice dogs will be expected to be able to handle slightly more challenging entries; and the Open dog is expected to jump in anywhere and get on with it – if it runs up to the edge and launches itself into the water, top marks!

Sometimes the dog may decide to return by land, and in this case marks will not be deducted if the dog, by doing so, did not take more time than had it returned by water. On smaller ponds, it may be quicker for the dog to run back round the edge rather than swim back.

Delivery to hand is required and points will be deducted if the dummy is put down at the edge while the dog has a good shake, even if immediately afterwards it picks it up again and brings it to hand.

### Handling

The judge, while not directly judging the handler, will nevertheless take into account the input given over the course of the test at hand. Quiet handling will be appreciated (and not only by the judge, but also by all watching), and while marks may not actually be gained by quiet handling, marks may well be deducted for persistent loud handling whether by voice or whistle – or both. It is a fact that when things are not going to plan, many handlers start overhandling their dog, which may not help the dog, and which certainly won't help their marks if the judge decides enough is enough and starts methodically deducting points for each desperate yell.

### Duration of a Test

At all levels, the judge will allow a certain amount of time for a retrieve to be completed. This time is only really required when things are not going to plan and the judge has to make the call as to when it is really no longer productive for the attempt to be continued, when he may ask the handler to 'pick up please', or advise the handler that a last attempt may be made. The judge may also invite the handler to move forwards from his mark closer to the dog and the retrieve in order to ensure that the dog finally succeeds in the retrieve, albeit at the expense of having to record a zero mark.

How long the judge lets a retrieve go on is entirely their decision, but will take into account whether by persisting it is likely the retrieve can be made. There are all sorts of factors that may come into play here: scenting conditions may be bad, and are causing problems for the dog which is otherwise performing well; or the dog may have just moved up a class and while responding well to the handler, is just not quite going far enough but with a little coaxing could well succeed. These are just a couple of instances, but all kinds of situation may arise in which the judge has to make the call – often a difficult one. Of course the handler has the right to have a 'Good go' at any retrieve, but there does come a point at which a halt has to be called.

## THE FINAL RECKONING

At the end of the day, all the marks are collated and added up, which will yield the top performing dogs of the class. First, second and third places are recognized as being worthy of an award. In the event of a tie between one or more dogs, the one with the higher hunting mark takes precedence; but in the event of a tie over all four tests, a further run-off test will be held with the dogs concerned – though this is a very rare event indeed.

After the presentation ceremony, all the marks are displayed for each competitor to see; some societies put out the scores on a spreadsheet and are able to print out a score sheet for everyone to take home. Noting your own scores against those of the winning dogs (unless you happen to be the winning dog!) is highly useful: it allows you to identify where you fell short, and how far you fell short of the top performers – you now know (if you didn't already) which tests were weak and therefore need more work, and you also know the gap in your performance compared to the top ones – with a ten mark difference there is obviously a way to go. As you go through the season you can see how you are progressing, and this is one of the most valuable things about the working test: feedback for you to put into further training.

If you are puzzled about any of the results, the judges will be happy to explain them to you, and in doing so will give you useful tips as to how your own performance could be improved, as well as advice on aspects of your dog and its training needs.

### *Factors Affecting Performance*

### The Handler at Fault

In a surprisingly large number of cases the loss of points, or failure to complete a test, can be traced back to the handler, and not necessarily to the dog. Of course, the dog is the one out there doing the hard work, but success requires teamwork, and in a team of two, of which the dog is one, the other team member, the handler, has equal responsibility. In all too many cases, this simple arrangement is forgotten or is not appreciated in the first place: the dog is set off on this task, is unsure, loses confidence, and comes back having failed, without a word of help or encouragement from the handler, who then blames the dog. It is often the lament of gundog trainers that their real task is to train the handler and to a lesser extent the dog! At any working test you can witness the truth in this. At all levels of dog work, the handler must be actively engaged with the dog to ensure that the task is completed satisfactorily – the dog gains confidence, is flushed with pleasure at the praise it receives, and learns to trust its own instincts as well as the commands from the handler.

When practising at home or with the local gundog group the handler is among friends and under no competitive pressure. Come the working test, and the pressure mounts, particularly for the beginner. Lots of people are watching your efforts, and you, of course, want to do well and not look a fool in front of your fellow competitors. If things go well, you quickly overcome the stage fright and start to enjoy the whole day much more. It's when things start to go wrong that handlers can start to behave in the most peculiar ways – shouting louder (because the dog obviously can't hear), or giving a different command (the dog didn't understand the previous command, so I'll have to say it differently), which doesn't help the dog at all, but simply provides much amusement to the onlooker. We've all done it, and it can be tremendously difficult to restrain oneself from 'helping' the dog.

You need to *relax*, to judge when to give the dog another command or direction, and when it is best to leave it alone to get on with it. Sent out on a seen retrieve, the only command should be the one that sends the dog out for the retrieve. Judges are looking for the minimum of intervention by the handler, and appreciate quiet handling. On a blind retrieve it will be necessary to handle the dog, but it doesn't have to be done with a loud voice, or any voice at all – that's why we have hands and a whistle, and have done all that work in the training field learning how to use them and teaching the dog to understand them. It is often said that any nervousness, tension or panic in the handler is transmitted 'down the lead' to the dog, and that this will affect its performance – so try and stay calm. Remember that once you've taken the lead off the dog at the commencement of a test you are not allowed to touch the dog until the test has been completed.

## Wind

The wind has a crucial role for the HPR, relying as it does on scent brought to it borne on the wind. For a dog to retrieve a dummy that it hasn't seen fall, it must be able to scent it from a distance for it then to be able to home in and make the retrieve. If you send your dog out on a line that takes it upwind of the dummy, you are immediately putting it at a huge disadvantage: it won't 'wind' the dummy, and you will have to intervene and handle it with whistle and hand signals into the area of the retrieve. Send the dog on a line that will result in it arriving in an area downwind of the retrieve: this gives it the best chance of picking up the scent and making a successful retrieve. All you had to do was send the dog. Brilliant: top marks, well done handler. Morale of the story: think about the wind. Before every retrieve, take stock of the scene, ascertain the direction of the wind, and plan how you wish the dog to make the retrieve. The effect of wind is treated in more depth in the chapter on field trials.

## Voice

The voice plays a bigger part in the success or failure of a retrieve than we would think. In basic training we learn to modulate our voice to impart encouragement with sweet, soft tones, and a harsher tone to impart displeasure and to signal to the dog to desist, or to tell it that it's doing something wrong. The proficient trainer and handler will switch voice tone in an instant to accord with the dog's behaviour. The speed of the switch is crucial, because a dog only relates what it hears from you to the action it is currently engaged in; therefore if it is doing something wrong it needs to be told *immediately* so it associates its action with your displeasure.

Leave it too long and the dog will associate the correction with its next activity – that is, what it is now engaged in – which may not be the action you are seeking to correct, which happened some moments ago.

You therefore need to be quick. An experienced handler will have a good idea of what can go wrong, and will have automatic responses that can be uttered immediately. Try to think ahead of the dog, because in doing so you will be in a better position to correct any error or mistake much faster than if you merely observe the proceedings, are surprised by an error, and then have to think what to do – all this is lost time.

Encouraging tones are easier to make when speaking softly, but often the dog needs to be commanded, and encouraged, at a distance. What often happens is we raise the voice in order to be certain that the dog can hear us, but we forget (or don't think) about imparting encouragement, ending up with what sounds (to the dog) like an angry shout. It requires a conscious effort to keep the voice neutral or sweet when we raise it.

Some dogs, particular younger ones, when faced with too many commands will simply give up. This is also true if the dog feels that it is doing the wrong thing by hearing what it thinks is a voice of displeasure.

Try the following at your training class: walk 150 yards away from the group, and have one of them command you as they would a dog. Even if they are shouting at the top of their voice, the chances are that you will have difficulty hearing them clearly – and this is even more difficult if there is a wind against you. Yet back with the dog, we expect that it is hearing us perfectly. True, a dog has better hearing, but the point is, the level of sound at 100 yards is surprisingly low – which is why we use hand signals.

## Hand Signals

Hand signals are extremely effective, and in particular over long distances – distances that your voice could not possibly make. This being the case, it doesn't make much sense to signal with your hand (which the dog can see) *and* with your voice (which it most likely can't hear): the hand signal is enough. When training a dog to understand hand signals we use a combination of voice and hand, but once it can understand and act on the hand signal, there is no need for the voice any more. Quiet handling will be credited by the judges.

## Whistle

The whistle should be used at an absolute minimum. It is so tempting to whistle the dog to get its attention to give it another command or hand signal, but over-use of the whistle may distract the dog unnecessarily, and may cause it to 'close down' and give up, simply because being whistled at every step, it feels it can't do anything right, and doesn't understand what is required of it. Get to this point and you have failed, the dog is discouraged, and its confidence dented.

## Insist on Success

If the test is too much for the dog or things are not going the right way, do not allow it to degenerate into failure. It is important that the dog has some measure of success, and it is of the utmost importance that it succeeds in making the retrieve even at the expense of scoring a zero mark. Be prepared to walk forwards (remember to ask the judge first) and help your dog make the retrieve – this is more important than the mark, because there will always be the next working test.

## Good Handling

A good handler will be quiet and will leave the dog to get on with its task, only intervening when absolutely necessary. It takes a lot of practice and experience to reach the point where you can be confident of your dog in its ability to carry out any one task, and to know when it needs your help, and when to shut up and leave

*Holding on to the retrieve while having a shake is good dog work.*

it alone. On the other hand, it is also the sign of a good handler who corrects the dog immediately they see something is not going quite right – for example, if the dog sets off on a different line to that which you indicated. The correct action is to stop the dog, bring it back and send it again, this time on the line that you want. It is much less satisfactory to let it continue, either in the hope that it will eventually find its way to the area of the retrieve, or by handling it by means of whistle and hand signal.

## Testing the Boundaries

'I can't understand it, he always does this perfectly at home!' This is the horrified observation

made by many an exasperated handler to the judge, or to fellow competitors, when his dog has just completely messed up. However, the working test environment is very different from the home training field, with many more dogs present and a completely different atmosphere, different smells and all sorts of distractions. Your dog will hear encouragement, exasperation, anger, despair being voiced by other owners, and may have to wait quite a long time on the lead before its turn comes round. The waiting can wind some dogs up to such a pitch of frustration/excitement that when it is their turn, they are so euphoric at being off the lead that they completely forget about anything other than being free and having a good run. Retrieve? What retrieve?

You cannot correct your dog at a working test: mild admonishment is acceptable, but harsh correction is not tolerated and may well result in you being asked to leave the ground. Dogs work this out very quickly for themselves, particularly the younger dog who is anyway always testing the boundaries with his owner to see what he can get away with; the working test is therefore the perfect environment for him to push and test the envelope a little further.

Puppies, by and large, are generally just enthusiastic and playfully unaware of doing any wrong; they aren't being awkward, but the excitement of the new situation and the many other young dogs in the class just gets too much for them. It's the older, more experienced ones that can play up, because they have learned that the teenage rebellion goes unchallenged and they can get away with it. Some appear to play up to it, and the owner becomes increasingly certain that the dog is behaving in this way deliberately, just to show him up in front of the crowd. However, it is highly unlikely that the dog is thinking this: it just knows it can get away with it at a working test.

Frankly, there is no solution to this, and it generally sorts itself out as the training at home progresses, and as the dog becomes more used to the working test environment, so that going to completely new venues becomes less of an excitement. All dogs, no matter what their level, can still be afflicted by unexplained deviations from their normal behaviour or performance, leaving the owner wondering just what is going on. But the vital thing to remember is to remain calm and not get caught up in an emotional battle of wills with your dog – though this is maybe easier said than done.

At the end of the working test, after the presentation of awards, the judges are asked to pass comment on the performance of their class. Time and again, the same comments on handling are made; the most frequent are described below.

## The Judge's Comments

### Mixed Commands/ Too Many Commands

The panicked handler starts to mix up commands, or to invent new ones (clearly the others are not working); for example, a simple 'Back' command, ignored or misunderstood by the dog becomes 'Go back, back, go on, go back, back, *no!* get on back!' and so on.

'Back', 'Go back', 'Go on' and 'Get on' as commands may be fine on their own, and used in the appropriate context: the first two are employed to get the dog to move in a direction directly away from the handler, while 'Go on' is employed to encourage the dog to keep going – but 'Go on back', while having the obvious meaning to the reader, will simply muddle a dog, already confused by the barrage of words and which has in all probability given up trying to please.

### Too Much Whistle

This is the classic situation where a retrieve is going wrong and the handler tries desperately to control every step the dog makes. Some experienced handlers still have a tendency to do this – even knowing that they do it, but really shouldn't. Much better just to back off or use the whistle to sit the dog still where it is for half a minute, which allows the handler to take stock of the situation and decide what needs to be done.

### Loud Handling

Self-evident you would think, but some handlers simply don't seem to be aware that they are bellowing their instructions.

### Not Helping the Dog

The opposite to over-handling is not stepping in to help the dog when it is looking to you for some guidance. This can be because the handler is trying so hard to be a quiet handler and thereby gain the judge's approval that he overdoes it,

*Just downwind of the retrieve, the dog scents its quarry.*

to the extent of not saying anything and having the dog fail. Often this is an inexperienced handler faced with a new situation that they don't know how to solve.

The misuse of the 'Hi lost!' and 'there' commands falls into this category: 'Hi lost' tells the dog that it is in the vicinity of the retrieve and that it should start hunting around in that area.

Note the word 'vicinity': too many handlers send their dog out and immediately start crying 'Hi lost, hi lost' even though the poor animal is nowhere near the retrieve area. 'There' is used to indicate that the dog is very, very close to the retrieve, being almost upon it. With the handler yelling 'Hi lost, hi lost, there, there, hi lost' the dog is being hindered, not helped.

# Chapter 9

# Spring Pointing

As the name suggests, spring pointing events are held in the spring, from March onwards through to May, even June, depending on the height of the crops. These events are really intended for young HPRs to gain their first experience of field work and pointing, and were introduced in 1982 as a way of improving the quartering performance. Set usually on wheat, barley or rape, the ideal time is when the crop is just high enough to be tempting feeding for the local game birds and capable of 'holding'

them – that is, the birds feel the crop is high enough to provide them with protection, and so are happy to stay in it feeding, rather than moving away from it. This provides the HPR with game to be located and pointed. As we are out of the shooting season, game can be found and pointed, but not shot, and so the spring pointing rules emphasize game finding. With cereal or rape fields or the grouse moors we generally have very large expanses of field that are absolutely perfect for the HPR to show off its

*Competitors at a spring pointing test.*

*Young Weimaraner on point.*

quartering abilities, running wide and far in search of its quarry. This is the HPR at its best, spectacular to watch.

Events are held by the HPR breed societies, from whom entry forms and schedules can be obtained. There is no formal limit to the number of dogs that can take part, but a practical limit, imposed by the available daylight, is fifteen dogs. If there is to be a ballot due to more entries than available places, preference is usually given to dogs under two years of age; additional preference may also be given to dogs of the breed of the society promoting the event. Suffice to say, if you have a young dog you can pretty much expect to get a run.

Two judges are appointed: one is usually a Kennel Club field trial judge on either the 'A' or 'B' panel; the other can be another panel judge, or a so-called non-panel, or learner judge, because judging a spring pointing event is one of the first appointments for the aspiring field trial judge. Although KC judges are normally used, spring pointing events are not run under Kennel Club rules.

Dogs are run singly for not less than ten minutes, and should always be directly into wind to foster the best quartering pattern, with each dog getting two runs, one in the morning and then again in the afternoon (unless eliminated). Quartering in search of game, a successful find and a staunch point is a credit with the judges, but the emphasis in judging is very much on the quartering – the hunting ability – of the dog, specifically the ground treatment and correct head carriage for the breed. Correct ground treatment, with the dog methodically working its beat, is most important. If the dog is covering the ground correctly, not missing ground, ranging the same distance on either side of the handler, with its nose in the air, then it is putting itself in the best position to be able to scent and point any game present. The hunting style of the dog will be noted – the correct head carriage is important for the air-scenting dog, the drive with which it goes about its task, and whether it turns into the wind at the end of its beat. Some dogs, particularly youngsters, may turn downwind – 'Back casting' – an undesirable feature which is untidy and inefficient.

Coming on to point, the handler will be asked by the judge to command the dog to flush the bird, and the judge will note the style of the flush and, most importantly, the steadiness of the dog – it must sit as soon as the bird lifts. At this time of the year partridge will be pairing up, so it's a good bet that if one partridge gets up or is flushed, its mate will be very close by – so be extra careful in making sure that the immediate area is covered by the dog, especially the edges of the field if they are not too far away, and be mindful of the wind direction to ensure the dog is on the right side of it. It often happens that the handler, having had a point and flush on a single partridge, and having walked forwards to handle the dog from the point to the flush (and proud of the good work done, with the warm feeling of a good grading being awarded), then sets the dog off hunting up the field again – but leaving the ground behind uncovered. And then the other partridge takes flight, but behind the dog now, and he is eliminated for missed game – and so the chances of a grading are lost, and the good work up until that moment is thrown away. This is purely a handling fault.

A successful run with a point and flush with the dog steady will result in the judges being able to 'grade' the dog. They will tell you immediately at the end of your run that you've been 'graded', though they will not tell you which grade has been awarded – that will come only at the end. If a grade has been awarded on the first run, the dog may improve on its grade on the second run, but the original grading is not lost if the dog is eliminated on the second. Eliminating faults are:

- not hunting;
- chasing game;
- not holding a point – running in;
- unsteady to flush.

As each dog is run for ten minutes with two runs in the day and with about fifteen dogs to run (if not eliminated at some point), it is clear that a huge amount of ground needs to be available on which to hold the event – one dog alone could quite easily cover twenty to thirty acres on a single run – so large farms with contiguous adjoining fields are used. It is rare indeed, even on field trial venues, to have access to large areas of ground on which to run the HPR, so spring pointing events are one of the few times that the dog will be able to run far and wide, and are consequently very popular events.

At the end of the day, the judges confer, and the gradings they have awarded are announced. Gradings are 'Good', 'Very Good' and 'Excellent'. Younger dogs are graded on pheasant and partridge, while those over two years old can be graded only on the much harder-to-find partridge. Just for fun, an award is often made for the best chase of the day in the opinion of the fellow competitors.

## GROUSE POINTING

Grouse pointing events are run along the same lines as spring pointing, but take place on the grouse moors where grades may be awarded for points on grouse only. It is worth noting here that although the scent of the grouse is quite strong, it is quite different to that of the pheasant and partridge with which the average HPR usually comes into contact, such that grouse may not be immediately pointed by those with no previous experience of them. This is particularly true for the older dog, which may need a day or longer to work out they should be pointing the scent. Therefore it is a good plan to take your youngster up to the moors as soon as is practicable – though do bear in mind that running over the heather is very hard going, and possibly too much for a very young dog.

## WHERE TO GO

Not all the breed societies run spring or grouse pointing events, so some research on the web sites is necessary. However, most of the field trial secretaries of any of the societies will know of them, even if they are not running one themselves.

# Chapter 10

# Field Trials

A field trial is a competitive event run in the manner of a rough shooting day, in which the performance of the dogs is judged, and for which awards may be given for the best performances. If you aspire to your dog becoming a field trial champion, able to use the prized 'Ft. Ch.' prefix, this is where you need to be. Although field trials are held for all the sub-groups of gundog, we are concerned only with the HPR trials.

Field trials are run under Kennel Club rules (J) by the breed societies and other gundog clubs licensed to hold field trials, and are organized into stakes: Novice, All-Aged and Open. You start off in the Novice trials, and progress through All-Aged to the Open trials, which represent the highest level and are where field trial champions can be 'made up'.

The starting point is the Novice stake, open to those dogs that have not gained a first in a

*Field trial competitors wait their turn.*

Novice stake, or an award in an All-Aged or Open stake. The All-Aged stakes are open to all dogs (although preference may be given to those with field trial awards), and are seen as a stepping stone to the Open trials; they are judged as an Open trial would be judged, but without the possibility to 'qualify'. Open trials are open to all dogs of the required standard. Win first place in an Open trial, and your dog has a 'leg up' to being a field trial champion; if it achieves another first, then the dog will be 'made up' to be a Ft. Ch. Winning a first or second in an Open trial qualifies the dog to take part in a Championship Stake. As you would expect, to achieve a first in an Open trial requires the dog to perform beautifully on the day, perfectly executing its tasks over the two runs: and this, as we shall see, is a real achievement indeed.

Field trials are not for everyone – although intended to be run as closely as possible to a normal rough shooting day, they are in reality highly structured events quite often very far removed from the ordinary rough shoot; nevertheless they are testing, demanding the very best performance from your dog to win a coveted field trial award at any of the stakes. And by training your dog to perform at the standard required in a field trial, you will have a dog to be proud of, and one that will stand out as an exceptionally useful addition to any shooting party or shoot. Those who take part in field trials travel all over the country, sometimes setting off very early indeed to drive three or four hours to the venue, in the knowledge that there is a distinct possibility that the dog could be eliminated in seconds for some misdemeanour, when it would be out of the trial completely. It does happen, thankfully not too frequently, and it does demand a very philosophical approach, to be able to shrug one's shoulders and look forward to the next trial.

All the hard work, disappointments and misfortunes are forgotten, however, when you experience the euphoria of winning your first award, with the attendant life qualification to enter the field trial classes at Crufts and entry in the Kennel Club stud book. You never forget the ground, who the judges were, and how your dog ran. HPR field trials are noted for their good humour and sportsmanship, and in the company of twelve other like-minded individuals – many of them real characters, those who have made up field trial champions, and professional gundog trainers, but all committed to the HPR – you will certainly have a real day out, and the best opportunity to listen, watch and learn with the best in the sport.

The basic format of a field trial consists of twelve dogs that are run singly for about ten minutes, one after the other, under the direction and watchful eyes of two judges accompanied by guns – up to four persons whose sole task is to shoot game for the dogs to retrieve. The dogs are required to hunt and point any game that is found, flush the game into the air when directed, being steady to shot and fall, and finally retrieving the game to hand. Dogs are run twice if they are not eliminated. Those who have completed the hunt, point and retrieve successfully are invited to complete a final retrieve out of water, and at the end may be the lucky recipients of a field trial award. As you might expect, however, it is rarely that simple!

## ENTERING A FIELD TRIAL

As we have seen, a field trial is run as one of three stakes: Novice, All-Aged and Open. A Novice stake is the starting point for all dogs, and you will continue to compete in Novice stakes until you become ineligible by virtue of winning one with a first place award. To enter a field trial you must obtain an entry form from the field trial secretary of the society running the event; they can usually be downloaded from the web site as well. Send it, completed, to

*There are usually two to four guns at a trial.*

the field trial secretary by the published closing date. Note that for most societies the entry forms must be in the hands of the field trial secretary on that date, to be eligible for entry into the trial or the draw; entries postmarked with the closing date will be too late and not considered. It is important to check the schedule for the trial, and to read the standing instructions issued by the society, which will contain the relevant information.

More and more entries are being processed online with all the cost advantages, the automation of the process and, of course, less paper.

Some systems will take the entry fee after the trial has taken place and the run is confirmed, others require payment on the day.

After the closing date, the field trial secretary will collate all the entries, and if there are more than twelve (the maximum number of dogs that can run in a trial), a ballot takes place, with the first twelve out of the hat being given a run. Any remaining entries will continue to be drawn to make up a list of reserves.

The field trial secretary then conveys the result of the draw to all entrants. The reserve list is important: handlers withdraw their dogs for a variety of reasons – for example, a bitch coming into season cannot run in the trial and must be withdrawn, or a dog may be injured, or may have won another trial, making it ineligible for this trial. On the day of the trial itself, if a handler and dog fail to appear by the time the trial is declared to have started, they will lose their place and it will be offered to the next dog on the reserve list that is present and ready to go. It is amazing how quickly the reserve list can be used up, with a dog drawn as fourth reserve and no apparent hope of gaining a run, suddenly called upon as others have withdrawn before the trial, moving it up to first reserve – and then, on the day of the trial, because you bothered to turn up and someone else didn't, you are able to run your dog.

If an online system is being used to manage entries then the procedures described above are taken care of by the software and generally makes life a lot easier for the Secretary.

## TRIAL DAY

On the trial day itself it is important to be on time! You should arrive well before the published start of the trial, usually 9am, planning your journey with sufficient leeway in case of accidents, traffic jams and the other 101 things that can make driving a frustrating experience. At most trials there will be limited space to exercise, so it is a good idea to find somewhere beforehand to let your dog(s) out.

The chief steward is responsible for the smooth running of the day, and you should make yourself known to them, and obtain your armband with the number corresponding to your place in the running order. You will also receive a printed programme containing the running order, and any changes that have been made up to that point. At 9am the chief steward will call everyone together to welcome them to the trial, and will then determine whether all the handlers and dogs that have been allocated a run are present, and if not, call up any reserves that are there. This done, the judges, the guns, the picking-up dog and the red flag are all introduced. The judges are asked to make their opening remarks. Moving off, the steward will usually call for the first three dogs to come up, and the first dog to run will go straight on up to the judges to start immediately; the steward always has the next two in the running order up with him, to go on up behind the judges so they can be called up promptly to the line without delay. The rest of the field (the gallery) follow at a safe distance grouped behind the person designated with the red flag.

For those further down the running order it is valuable to observe the dogs running in front of you as closely as possible. Take the opportunity to notice the direction of the wind, and do so regularly as it may well change. You will be able to assess the scenting conditions and the amount of game, whether it is plentiful with a dog quickly coming on point, or whether dogs are having to hunt hard to find anything.

## MANAGING YOUR RUN

To be successful in a trial and gain an award, the judges must be able to record that a dog can hunt, point the game that it finds, and retrieve shot game to command: the 'H', 'P' and 'R' boxes need to be ticked. The best demonstration of this is the dog that hunts and finds game, points it, flushes it on your command, and is steady to the flush, shot and fall of the bird, which it subsequently retrieves. Such an HPR, all completed in sequence and perfectly executed, will impress the judges the most and give you the chance of gaining a good placing in the awards, even winning the trial. You may not be able to complete the sequence in one go: the dog may hunt incredibly well, but not find any birds to point; it could find a bird, point and flush it correctly, but the bird is missed by the guns, so while the 'hunt' and 'point' parts have been ticked, the dog did not have the opportunity of a retrieve. It may be that you are called up to do a retrieve (perhaps because the dog before you has failed) before you have had the chance to run: success here will mean that you will be credited with the retrieve, but still have the hunt and point to complete. The 'H', 'P' and 'R' can be done in any sequence.

Many handlers new to field trials feel that the best outcome is a blank first run, with no excitement, the dog hunting happily but not finding anything. This is down to nerves, and the thought of them having to deal with a point and retrieve, with all the things that can possibly go wrong, leads them to believe that a quiet first run will give them time to settle down and get used to the idea of running a dog in a trial. This may well be the case, but the down side of this approach is that if the first run is indeed blank, it means more pressure on the second run, as there will then be the need to demonstrate everything on that run. The danger here, of course, is that there may well not be the opportunities to get the HPR that you need, and you are risking the outcome on just one single attempt. Experienced handlers try and get everything done on the first run: if something does go wrong, well, that's trialling and there is nothing to say that what went wrong on the first run would not have gone equally awry on the second.

On being sent forward to the judges by the steward, hang back a little if they are still conferring amongst themselves, until they indicate for you to come forward. The judges will check your number and then indicate to you the ground they wish you to cover, and the direction to go, and they will point out the extent of the beat they wish to see covered, if it is not obvious. They may say to take the guns on either side as the width of the beat the dog should run (this may be because they want to divide a field up into strips, and don't want your dog spoiling the ground that they plan to use for later dogs), or they may simply say 'there's the field, off you go'. If you are unclear as to what it meant, ask before you set your dog off. It is now up to you to decide how best to manage the beat with regard to the prevailing wind and other considerations, to notice pockets that will need covering or likely bushes to be checked.

## Where's the Wind?

The first thing to do is to determine the direction of the prevailing wind. With a stiff breeze it is an easy matter; more problematic is when there is little or no discernible breeze, or it appears to be swirling round. It can help to put a finger in the air, or to observe the smoke from a cigarette or from the smoke matches that plumbers and air-conditioning engineers use to detect airflow. Throwing a tuft of grass only works when the wind is sufficiently strong to be able to move it, which would be an airflow you should be able to detect anyway.

### Head Wind

As we have seen, the HPR hunts for game by quartering the ground in front of it, but as the scent it needs to locate game is carried on the wind, the dog has to position itself such that it has the best chance of catching a whiff of the quarry it is seeking. This is most evidently going to be directly downwind, and so the HPR will automatically adjust its running pattern so that it is at all times running across the face of the oncoming wind. It is easiest for the dog, and the most advantageous, when the wind is a head wind – that is, it is blowing directly into the face of the dog and handler when both are facing the field. Where at all possible, the

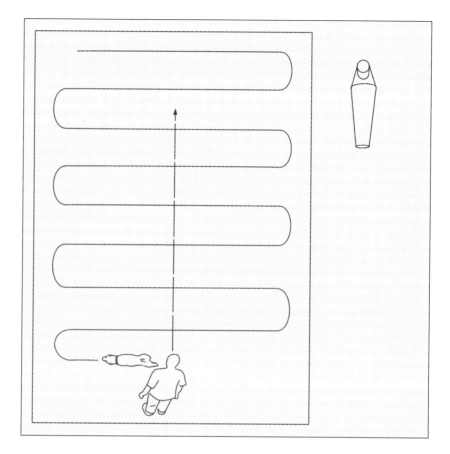

*The head-wind pattern is the most advantageous for the dog. Always try to run into wind.*

dog must be positioned so that it runs into the wind, especially the younger dog. At field trials the judges will do their utmost to ensure that, whenever possible, dogs are run into the wind at every level of field trial stake, although the All-Aged and Open level dogs should be capable of managing wind from any direction.

With a head wind, the handler in the company of the guns will move up the field in a line behind the quartering dog, which is also making its progress directly up the field, maintaining a regular quartering pattern, working from side to side running across the oncoming breeze.

## Back Wind

Running with a back wind is the least favourable wind direction, as scent is being blown away from the dog if it runs with the wind. The second disadvantage is that any noise made by the shooting party will be carried on the wind into the ears of the wary game bird, providing it with a timely early warning of danger approaching, and enabling it to make the very sensible decision to run away.

To counter the problem of the scent drifting with the wind away from his nose, the HPR adopts a different running strategy: first it will run out downwind away from you in a straight line until it is some distance away (200 yards or so), before turning to run across the wind and to start quartering, with the wind blowing directly towards it – it now has a head wind, and so can work its way back up towards you.

Dogs vary in their ability to work a back wind in the textbook fashion described above and in the diagram: some indeed may be incapable of making a good job of it, while others can execute it perfectly. Those less able can usually be improved through training.

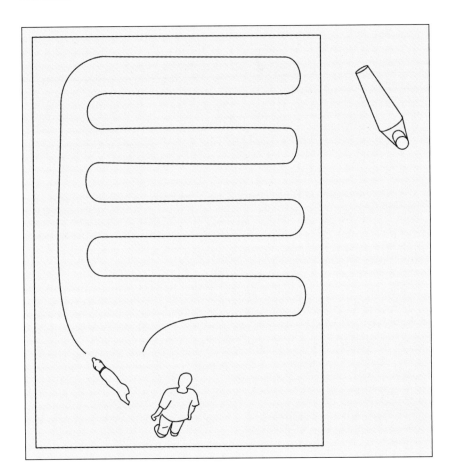

*Running a back wind is most difficult and should be avoided wherever possible.*

## Cheek Wind

As the name suggests, a cheek wind is felt on either one of the cheeks, and denotes a wind that blows at an angle to your face, round to 90 degrees (when it would be blowing on either side of the face). From the diagram opposite you can see the dog has altered its quartering pattern, such that it is still running across the face of the wind, resulting in it now running along a line that is at a slant to the original pattern. While the dog happily continues on its way, it is unaware that it is now running a longer beat than previously (assuming it continues to run from edge to edge, the new distance is equal to the length of the original beat divided by the cosine of the angle of wind change) – but we need to consider what happens when the handler turns to walk directly into the wind to follow the dog. He would now be heading to a point some way short of the end of the field, which is not where he wants to end up, and also, by doing so, he would no longer be walking in the middle of the dog's beat. Continuing on this line, one side of the dog's beat will be getting shorter and shorter until eventually there is nowhere to run. Not good. And look what else has happened – the handler is now at the upwind edge and in the worst possible place to continue.

The solution is for the handler, as soon as the cheek wind is noticed, to move towards the downwind edge of the field and walk along that. It may be a good idea to walk a short quartering pattern so the dog does not notice any difference in your movements compared to those it would normally expect. For the beginner, the cheek wind is often a difficult thing to come to terms with, especially when the wind changes in the middle of your run. If you are faced with

*The cheek wind is often encountered: note how the handler moves in relation to the dog.*

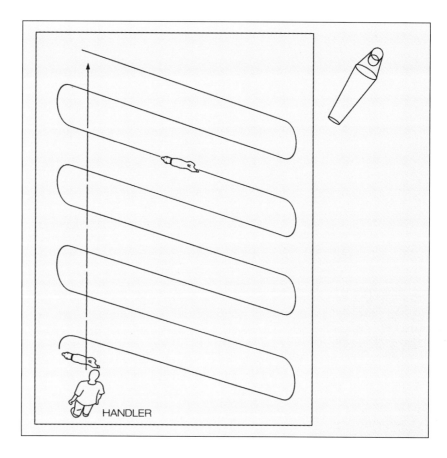

a cheek wind from the very start, take extra time to work out how you are going to approach the run – how the dog will run, and where you should be walking – and do remember to cast the dog off in the direction that will give it the longest run. As we've noted before, don't move forwards until the dog has crossed in front of you, ensuring the ground you are about to step into has been covered. Take some comfort from the fact that it's only you with the difficulty: the dog will just get on with it.

## Changing Wind

You should now have the idea that keeping tabs on what the wind is doing is important, not only at the beginning of the run when you take the time to work out where it is and how best to manage it, but also during the run itself. Once you've started, it is all too easy to forget about the wind as you get involved with watching the dog, managing the run to ensure good ground coverage, perhaps intervening to get a likely bush investigated, while watching where you are going. Furthermore, as you move forwards you create your own impression of wind – if you run forwards when it's dead calm you will feel wind pressure on your face – and your movement will give rise to your sensing the apparent wind direction, which may well be different to the actual wind direction.

As we've seen, the dog will adjust its hunting pattern according to the wind, so the best indicator of what is happening is to observe how it is moving to see if the angle of the pattern in relation to you has changed. This may not always be easy to see or work out, but simply standing still for a couple of moments is an easy way to check. Do remember, though, that what you feel on your face may not be what is happening down at the height of the dog's nose.

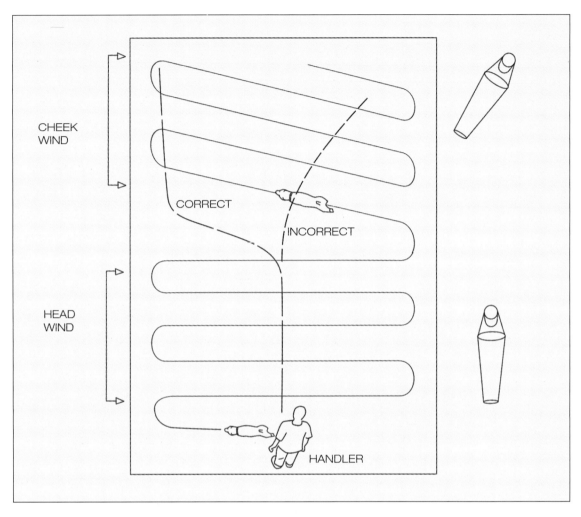

*A changing wind direction can catch you out. Always be aware of its direction, and be prepared for it to change.*

### Starting Your Run

Sit the dog and remove the lead. Take a moment to check the direction of the wind, and decide which way to cast the dog off and how you propose to work the beat given. As a beginner it is all too easy to forget all this in the excitement of being there – but take the time to do the basics. More experienced handlers will have checked out the beat and the wind on the way up to the judges, and will already have planned how to start their run. Try and do the same.

Once you have cast your dog off, do not move forwards at once, but wait until the dog has gone past you in front before advancing. The reason is this: if you move forwards immediately, you are moving into ground that has not yet been covered by the dog, and your forward movement will cause the dog, when it turns to come back past you, to take a line further forwards than it would have done had you stood still. In doing so, you have created an area of ground that will not be covered by the dog, but which could well still contain game. If game gets up from this ground the judges will terminate your run and the dog will be eliminated for missing game. You will not be comforted by the knowledge that this was caused by your error

*Once you have cast the dog off, don't move forwards immediately, or it will miss ground.*

---

## Awareness of the Wind

Awareness of the wind at all times is a good thing for any HPR handler when out on the shooting field, and we have already seen how the HPR reacts to the wind and the effect on the way it runs. In a field trial it is of paramount importance to read the wind correctly and be aware of how it will affect the dog's run, and the way it will cover the ground. Having assessed this, the handler must then make sure of walking in the right direction commensurate with the type of wind at hand. On the rough shoot, it may not matter if ground is not covered and a bird is missed or 'bumped', but in a field trial you will be eliminated if this happens – dog back on the lead and you are out, the end of your trial. In a field trial, your awareness of the wind is of the highest importance, much more so than at any other time when you are out with the dog.

While all HPR dogs react to the wind, some will make better use of it than others, and while the best game-finding dog is left alone just to get on with it, the less able may need a helping hand from you in ensuring they have covered their ground; alternatively you might alter your position relative to the dog so that it runs more advantageously. To get through a field trial, everything, absolutely everything, must be going your way, and to make this happen you must be on top of your game and alert to what is going on around you, as well as watching the dog like a hawk.

The novice handler is often surprised by the dog apparently running at a different angle than it was a minute ago – what has happened is the direction of the wind has changed, and the dog has automatically adjusted its run to maintain its line across the wind. Having missed this, the handler, who was walking along oblivious to the change, is now walking in the wrong direction. The dog, which usually has an eye on where the handler is, in adjusting its pattern to the new wind direction, has changed the angle at which it is running in relation to you, and you, not having made any change to your direction, could affect the length of the dog's beat such that it is not now covering ground as effectively as it was – now we are in the danger zone of a bird being missed, and therefore elimination. The novice handler cannot be expected to grasp all of these ramifications, and so mistakes will be made and you are sure to be eliminated; but the judges may explain to you what the mistake was, how it came to be, and what you should have been doing to avoid it – if they don't offer this advice, you can ask them what went wrong.

As we have already seen, the head wind is the easiest for the dog and handler to manage, and in a field trial, the judges are required by the 'J' regulations to run dogs into the wind, whatever the level of stake, wherever it is possible to do so. In a Novice trial, you should in theory always be run into a head wind, although the layout of the ground may make this a practical impossibility. The judges will have consulted with the local gamekeeper before the commencement of the trial to ascertain the best way round the trial ground, such that the majority of dogs can expect to experience a head wind. Nobody likes to run a back wind: the dog is put at an immediate disadvantage, and it is awkward for the handler to manage, not only his own movements but those of the guns as well.

Not all dogs can run a back wind well, and it is unlucky indeed for such a dog to be eliminated for a fault while trying to manage a back wind when it is an excellent performer otherwise. The most common problem is that when the dog has run out downwind and starts to work back up towards you into the wind, its quartering pattern is not as good this way round as it would be when working a head wind; so the handler now has to work hard with whistle and hand signal to get the dog to cover the ground properly, which is unpleasant and nerve-wracking to do.

If you have to run a back wind, cast the dog off and it will start its run straight out in front of you downwind. (Don't worry if the dog disturbs game on the outrun: as long as it acknowledges game so flushed, but carries on, it will not be penalized.) The key thing now is *not to move forwards* until the dog has covered the ground directly in front of you. The judges and guns should not move forwards either, and if they do, you are within your rights to ask them to stay where they are. Only when you are satisfied the ground has been covered should you then move forwards, walking briskly to the point at which the dog turned on the first downwind cast, as this is then the starting point of ground as yet uncovered.

The major difference to the handler is that the dog is now running its quartering pattern working progressively towards him. This does have the advantage that the dog can easily see any hand signals or upper body movement made to modify its pattern, or to cover ground indicated by the handler – but there is a very different picture if the dog goes on point. The situation is the dog is on point, say twenty yards away from you, in front and most likely facing towards you. Normally you would approach the dog from behind, but in this case you will need to move towards the dog along with the guns and the judges, in doing so walking over ground that has not yet been covered but which may well hold game that could be disturbed or flushed. You or the dog could not be penalized if game were disturbed in this way.

---

and not the poor dog, and is a classic beginners' error.

Faced with starting at the very edge of a field, it is a good plan to stand well back from the edge before casting off the dog to ensure that it has a chance to run along the edge and thereby cover this ground before advancing into the field proper. If you are running on a back wind, then you won't be moving forwards anyway, so it is less of a problem in this respect.

## *Working the Beat*

### Sugar Beet and Root Crops

Sugar beet is a fine crop in which to run an HPR, but is by no means the easiest, particularly for the younger or inexperienced dog. The large field sizes give ample opportunity to see the dogs ranging wide – all too rare nowadays, and a real treat for all. It is hard going for the dog (and for the human!), and the leaf cover provides the game bird with fantastic opportunities to run ahead unseen, and to double back behind the line of the quartering dog. The dog makes a great noise crashing through the crop, providing an excellent early warning to anything in front, which only encourages them to run on forwards. The noise also makes it more difficult for the dog to hear your whistle, some taking this as the perfect excuse not to listen! But for the dog that runs well and can keep up with the game sufficiently for it to stop running

*Root crops can be hard work!*

and crouch down to conceal itself, sugar beet gives the perfect opportunity for it to point and hold the birds fast.

### Game Cover

Most shoots grow some kind of game cover to feed and hold their birds, and these crops are very often encountered in trials. The upside is that there is a good chance of finding birds in them; the downside is that there may well be too many! In addition, early on in the season the crop may well be thick and high, making it very difficult to see what your dog is up to. Later on, when the cover becomes thinner, game crops can be the perfect ground on which to run. The watchword in higher and thicker game crops is to cover your ground: don't let the dog run on forwards unchecked, but make sure that it is working ground to left and right, and keep it working as close to you as possible. Use the whistle if you have to – judges appreciate quiet

handling, but given the choice between the judges' appreciation and being eliminated from the trial because you didn't keep your dog under control and covering its ground, the choice is clear: use the whistle. It is worth remembering that the judges can only judge the dog on what they can actually see, so working under these conditions can either work for you (the dog does something wrong, but gets away with it because it is out of sight), or against you (your dog actually does some wonderful work, but it goes unseen and cannot be credited).

If the dog just runs straight in front of you down to the end, flushing birds all over the place, you have not just ruined your own chances of succeeding in the trial, you have also ruined the chances of those behind you. Proceed with caution, and work the dog methodically down the strip, making sure the edges are covered. This is particularly important if the game cover has a hedge line on one side – you must get your dog to check the hedge regularly. If you don't, you run the double risk of missing a bird and being eliminated by the judges for not covering your ground. Slow down as you approach the end: any birds pushed forwards will be waiting until the very last moment before flying, so you actually have the best chance of your dog being able to hold a bird on point, as long as you are very careful that none of the other birds is frightened into the air by its approach, or your own.

Getting your dog to flush the bird it's pointing may well result in any number of others being flushed at the same time, and the resulting volley of fire from the expectant guns, coupled with the flurry of flushing birds, may all be too much for your dog, who, in its excitement, may either take it into its head to run in and see if there are any more that need pushing up, or take off to retrieve a shot bird. In any event, you will be out. So be ready, with whistle and voice, to make absolutely sure that the dog sits immediately the commotion starts – make sure it listens to you, distracting its attention away from what is happening around it – you must be

concentrating 100 per cent on your dog – and don't you be distracted by the spectacle, either! It's easier said than done, but this is one of the most tense, but equally potentially rewarding moments in a field trial, where the steadiness of your dog is being tested to the limit, and you cannot fail to impress the judges if you and the dog get it right.

## Open Woodland

Open woodland – with trees spaced a good distance apart, leaves underfoot, and some kind of bushy cover, rhododendron for example – makes excellent ground on which to run an HPR, and most like running on it. The key thing here, as with any run, is to make sure the beat you are given is covered completely: don't be in a hurry to move forwards, and ensure that the dog doesn't go charging forwards, taking too big a bite while quartering. Any clump of cover, or a fallen tree with its branches and leaves, needs to be investigated, and any dog worth its salt will do this automatically – your job is to oversee this work, and to ensure that if anything is missed, you direct the dog to make the ground good.

Remember that pheasant prefer to remain closer to the edge of the wood, and are more likely to be found in an area from the edges to about twenty-five to thirty feet in; they are far less likely to be found in the middle, so it is imperative that the edges, and right up to the very edge, is covered – it happens time and again on a trial that a dog turns fractionally short of the edge of the wood, up goes a pheasant, and you are eliminated.

In wet or damp woodland with bracken, woodcock are likely to be found, and a point on a woodcock is a good find indeed. Unfortunately for the competitor, they make a very difficult target to hit: small and fast with a jinking, low flight pattern, it takes a very good shot to hit one of these birds. Some dogs don't like the taste of them, and are reluctant to retrieve them or will not retrieve them at all.

## Hedges

Hedgerows are frequently encountered on field trials, as they are on any kind of rough shoot, and when running into a head wind working them is straightforward: let the dog off and let it get on with it. It is rare that the wind is blowing directly down the hedge line: more usually it will be blowing at some angle to it, and so through it. The dog will automatically put itself on the lee side of the hedge – that is, the side not facing the wind – and will work up the hedge line with the wind carrying the scent to it. This could be a problem if you have positioned yourself on one side of the hedge and the dog has decided the other side is better for it, leaving you without sight of your dog and unable to do anything if it happens to go on point. The better option would be to work out on which side the wind is coming through the hedge before you start the run; you can then position yourself correctly from the beginning.

It is perfectly acceptable to discuss your positioning with the judges, who in any case will also have to make a similar decision, because it is usual to have one judge on each side of the hedge along with a gun. While the judges will be following on behind, each gun should be briefed to walk just in front of the working dog, but out about ten to fifteen yards from the hedge itself. With an eager, fast working dog they may have their work cut out just keeping up, but you as the handler should determine the rate of progress and proceed at no more than a reasonable walking pace.

It may be tempting to whistle back a dog that has gone on too far ahead, but be careful not to disturb a dog that could well be intent on heading off a bird running up the middle of the hedge, as they very often do.

Working a hedge on a back wind requires a slightly different technique: the dog runs away from you down the hedge line with the wind behind it, so it is at an immediate disadvantage in terms of being able to scent game. The trick here is to let it run for 100 yards, say, and then pip it on the whistle to make it run back towards you so that it is now running into the wind.

**Flushing in the Hedge:** A dog may well move into the middle of the hedge if it can and move up behind the game in front, not always the best strategy as it merely serves to push them on faster, but sometimes they can be held on a point in the middle of the hedge, particularly if they have encountered an obstacle. Commanding the dog to flush the bird may result in it running fast along the middle of the hedge with the bird in front: this will not be penalized by the judges as chasing game, as long as the dog sits as soon as the bird takes to the air, by coming out of the hedge on one side and flying. Remember, it is the job of the dog to present the bird to the guns by getting it to fly.

### Tramlining, Roding In

Tramlining, or roding in, is the term given to the situation where the dog is following a strong foot scent, lowering its head and running fast in a straight line down the field – often down the wheelings or tramlines. It creates a headache for the handler, firstly because it may go a very long way away and not be productive: it doesn't find or point any game, then has to be brought all the way back to work the ground it had not covered before it took off. If it doesn't come back exactly the way it came, and as it is now running downwind, there is the danger of it running into and bumping game, which would result in elimination.

The second option is that the dog goes a long way and then goes on point. The problem here is that if the dog does not produce a bird from this point (if it is non-productive) then you and the guns and the judges have trailed all the way up to it, leaving a large amount of uncovered ground. If the dog does produce, all well and good; if not, you must go all the way back to where you were, with guns and judges, before this episode occurred, and cover the ground missed.

*Make sure you cover your ground, going back if necessary to take in ground missed.*

You are well within your rights when this happens to ask the gallery and the guns to stay where they are, and to consult with the judges quickly to agree how many guns to take up to the dog; make sure that this mini party stays close together to minimize ground disturbance. As you get nearer to the dog, fan out so as not to push the dog on to the bird. If the point turns out to be unproductive, or if the bird is not shot following a successful flush, then you will have to collect the guns and judge together and walk back with the dog to the others (being careful to leave uncovered ground as undisturbed as possible), and then to continue up the field again in order to cover the missed ground.

## POINTING AND FLUSHING

### On Point

If your dog is on a staunch point it is usual practice to raise one's hand to indicate the fact to the judges and 'claim the point'. Often the judges can see this for themselves, but there may be situations (for example if the dog is working in cover) when it is not obvious, and by raising the hand you alert them to the fact that they need to make their way towards you so they are in a position to verify the point, and so they can assess what comes next. The handler should approach the dog from the side so it can become aware

*On point.*

of you coming nearer, but is not frightened or 'spooked'. A dog on point can be just on the edge of moving in on the bird, and you don't want to do anything that may cause this to happen – which approaching from directly behind undoubtedly will. If you are not sure that your dog will be completely steady on point, blowing your whistle very gently as you come closer can reinforce its steadiness. Your goal is to be as close to the dog as possible.

It is the responsibility of the handler to arrange the positioning of the guns, but in practice it is rarely necessary, as in the main those who are invited to shoot at a field trial are experienced and know how to position themselves. The more experienced handler may wish to fine-tune the positions and is at liberty to do so. The pincer arrangement is most frequently employed, with one gun on either side of the dog on point, away from it by about ten yards

and slightly in front. With the dog pointing a bird directly ahead of it, the angle of its nose to the ground gives an indication as to its distance, which may require the position of the guns to be adjusted forwards or backwards. With a cheek wind or back wind blowing from one side, the dog may end up on point with its nose at right angles to the body, or even pointing slightly backwards: in this case the arrangement of the guns will be different, because the flight of the bird will be different as the flush will be pushing the bird out to the right or left (depending upon which way it is pointed), or even backwards.

### The Flush

With the dog still on point, and the guns arranged as required, one of the judges will indicate to the handler that the dog should be sent in to flush the bird into the air. The handler will initiate the flush by telling the dog to 'get in', or by simply clicking the fingers. It will race forwards, the sudden movement and fast approach leaving the bird with no alternative but to take to the air in order to escape.

A bird will normally try to take off into the wind because the extra airflow will generate more lift, thereby enabling it to gain height most quickly (aircraft always take off and land into the wind for the same reason). In most cases it will do just that, so you have a good idea that when the dog goes in and flushes a bird from directly behind, pushing it up into the oncoming wind, it will go up and forwards. However, these are wild animals that don't always behave as we might expect, and sometimes act against all logic (except their own).

The flush should be positive – that is, the dog moves in immediately on command, moving quickly to force the bird into the air. If a dog goes in too hard and too fast, however, with the bird just a short distance ahead, there is the danger that it will catch it before it has had time to lift: this is known as 'pegging' the bird. Dogs that are 'sticky' on point – that don't move off their point when commanded, or which take a tentative step forwards and stop, then require repeated urging to finally make the flush – will lose credit with the judges, as this constitutes a major fault.

Sometimes the bird will be invisible in the middle of some cover, bramble, thick hedge and so on. Here, the dog will be required to try and make the flush, and must be seen to make real attempts to penetrate the cover in order to do so. Dogs that just dance around the bush, or which refuse to try and penetrate the cover, may be eliminated. A dog that is seen to be doing its best by repeated attempts and by trying different points of entry, but is simply not able to penetrate the cover, will not be penalized, but the judges will take careful note of its

*Flush!*

efforts, and of the type of cover encountered. Credit will be given to the dog that perseveres and is finally successful in getting the bird out and into the air.

As soon as the bird lifts, with the characteristic sudden explosive whirring of its wings if it is a pheasant, the dog should stop and watch the bird fly away. It is not necessary for the dog actually to sit, although it is preferable, but it should be steady to the flush and any subsequent shot, not moving from where it was when the flush occurred. Any movement of the dog in the direction of the bird, and which may indicate unsteadiness, will be severely perceived by the judge, and may result in elimination. A dog that 'runs in' – sets off on a retrieve before being commanded (often wryly called an 'extended flush') – will be eliminated immediately.

## The Shot

The bird so flushed and in the air will take its chances with the guns present, whose job it is to get the bird on the ground, stone dead, for the dog to have the chance of a retrieve. A sporting shot is required: if the bird is shot too quickly it may suffer significant damage to the carcass, making an unpleasant retrieve for the dog and rendering the bird useless for the table; but more importantly, a bird shot at too close a range will result in a retrieve that is of little or no value in testing the dog, requiring a further bird to be available to it at some later point in the trial so that its retrieving ability can be tested to the satisfaction of the judges. In addition, a bird falling in front of the dog's nose, tempting it to unsteadiness, is plain unfair to the dog,

*The judge gives the handler a 'Mark' on a blind retrieve at a field trial.*

*Bringing the bird in nicely to hand looks good and will impress the judges.*

particularly in a Novice stakes. The ideal shot occurs when the bird has gained some height and is about twenty yards or more away.

## RETRIEVING

Assuming the flushed bird has been successfully brought back to the ground and with the dog steady, one of the judges will ask the handler to 'send your dog'. In the case that the dog has seen the bird fall and has had the opportunity to mark the point of fall, the judges will simply expect the handler to command the dog to make the retrieve. If the bird is down but the dog could not be expected to have seen or marked the point of fall – for example, after flushing, the bird flew over a hedge to be shot out of sight of the dog – the judges will ask the handler to

recall the dog, and then to accompany them to a point from which they require the retrieve to be started.

You will then be given a 'Mark' by the judges: that is, they will point out the area in which they believe the retrieve will be found. Take time to assess the retrieve, whether obstacles are involved, and be certain to check the wind so that you send the dog out on the best line. You will make the best impression on the judges if your dog goes straight out to the mark, picks up the bird and comes straight back without any delay. You will not be penalized on a blind retrieve for handling your dog into the area, but it should go out in a straight line in the direction you indicate – it doesn't look good if your dog charges off right or left and you have to start handling it immediately. The important thing, however, is to make the retrieve no matter how much handling it takes. As long as you do this, you will be asked to continue, with the manner of the retrieve only coming into the judges' deliberations at the end when they are making up their minds about what awards to give to which dogs. Clearly, a dog that performs the retrieve easily with no fuss or with minimal handling will, if other things are equal, be worthy of a higher award.

The delivery of the bird should be to hand. The main reason for this is that the bird may be a runner, or still alive, so if it is simply dropped in front of you, it may well jump up, run away or fly off, which means it will have to be retrieved again, causing unnecessary delay and distress to the bird, which should have been dispatched promptly. It looks much more polished and competent if the dog brings the bird gently

to hand, releasing its grip as you take hold of the bird.

It is worth noting here that it is usual in Novice stakes that game will not be shot while a dog is already out on a retrieve, and the guns will have been briefed on this by the judges prior to the commencement of the trial. In All-Aged and Open stakes the dog will be expected to ignore any such game taken and carry on with the retrieve it has been sent for.

### 'Eye Wiping' another Competitor

If a dog fails to make a retrieve after a reasonable amount of time looking for it in the right area, the judges may ask the handler to 'pick up' the dog, and will then call up the next dog in line to try for the retrieve. If this dog is successful it

*The retrieved bird must be passed to the judge.*

*All birds must be checked
by the judges for damage.*

will have 'wiped the eye' of the previous one, which will now be eliminated from the trial. If, however, this dog also fails, the judges may call up the next dog (and if this is successful it will have eye-wiped the preceding two, which are now eliminated). Failure here will usually result in the judges going forwards themselves to try and locate the retrieve. If they fail to find it, all the dogs that were tried are reprieved; but if they do find it, the dogs will be eliminated.

It is entirely at the judges' discretion as to how many dogs are tried in this manner – usually it is two, but there is nothing to stop the judges potentially calling up every dog on the card to try.

### Checking the Bird

The retrieved bird should be immediately passed to the judges, who will check that it is undamaged. If it is found to be undamaged, then you will be asked to continue your run, or you may be asked to pick up your dog and return to the gallery if the judges feel that you have done enough, or if you had come to the end of your allotted time.

If they consider the bird to be damaged in some way, they will tell you, and you do have the right to check the bird for yourself; however, you do not have the right to challenge their decision if you happen not to agree. If you are very new to trialling, you probably won't know how to check a bird anyway, so just accept the decision and go with good grace; indeed, this is by far the best way even if you are very experienced.

The judges check the bird by feeling for the ribcage and carefully checking its condition: if the ribs are damaged, stove in or broken, this is evidence of a hard mouth or harsh handling by the dog, and constitutes grounds for elimination. Of course, birds can be damaged by other factors, such as the bird being shot too close, and high birds may sustain damage by the force of impact with the ground. An experienced judge, however, will be able to tell damage that can be attributed to the dog, although it can be a very difficult call to make. If there is any doubt in the judge's mind, benefit must be given to the dog.

You are prohibited by the regulations from handling any game shot during the course of the trial.

### The End of the Run

At the end of the run, which should be at least ten minutes in length (longer at the discretion of the judges), the judges will ask the handler to 'pick up please', when you must recall your dog and put it on the lead. As soon as these words have been uttered, the judging of the run is at an end. If they don't say anything more to you, then you can assume that you are still in the trial (if you had made any eliminating faults then you would have been dismissed immediately after

the event) and can look forward to a second run; this is confirmed if they happen to say 'We'll be seeing you again'. You can ask the judges if you are still in, and they will tell you, but it is reasonably safe to assume that if you have not been explicitly eliminated by them, then you are still in the trial.

They will then finish recording their mark or grade for the run in the judges' book they have for the purpose. In particular, they will note any point the dog may have had, and whether the point was productive or not. Any retrieves that were completed will have been recorded immediately after their completion (or not, as the case may be).

## ROUND TWO

Having completed the first round of the trial by running all the dogs, the judges will confer so they agree as to which dogs should take part in the second round of runs. They will then inform the steward, who in turn will inform the handlers by calling out the numbers of those dogs that have not been eliminated. These dogs then each have a second run, when they have the opportunity to achieve any HPR components that they had not yet been able to demonstrate.

On completing the second round of runs, the judges will confer again and decide which of the dogs that have not been eliminated, can be selected to complete the final phase of the trial: the water retrieve. They come to this decision by consulting their judging books, to establish and confirm which dogs have completed the HPR sequence. The numbers of the dogs to be taken to the water are then announced by the steward.

There may be circumstances when the water retrieves cannot take place on the day of the trial, and in this case any announcements of awards to be made are provisional. They are only confirmed when the dog has completed a water retrieve within a three-week period after

*The water retrieve must be completed.*

the date of the trial, at a suitable venue, and ratified in the presence of an 'A' panel judge, who will then sign the water certificate, which confirms the provisional awards.

## THE END OF THE TRIAL: AWARDS

Those dogs successfully completing their water test will be eligible to receive a field trial award. This could be a first, second, third or fourth place, or a certificate of merit (CoM). The judges are not under any obligation to award a particular place if they feel the required standard has not been met, and are quite at liberty to withhold a place. So for example, they may decide to award a first, a third and a fourth along with two CoMs, withholding the second place award; at another trial a single fourth might be awarded, or no awards at all.

The judges communicate their decision to the steward, who will then make arrangements for place certificates to be made out in the name of the dog, countersigned by the judges who will also sign a game certificate, which certifies to the Kennel Club that sufficient game was present during the trial.

Finally, the steward will call everyone together for the awards ceremony, when he will ask the judges to make any comments or observations about their day and the performance of the dogs and handlers. He will also thank the host for the use of the ground, the guns for their expertise, and the red flag and picking-up dog for their gift of time in fulfilling these inglorious but necessary functions.

*The judges confer.*

Those with awards will rejoice in their success, in the knowledge that they, in partnership with their dog, have successfully completed the most testing of any kind of trial. Those who were not lucky enough to make it this time will have learned a little more about trialling, themselves and their dog, which hopefully will help them be one of those in the awards at a future trial.

## HUNT, POINT, RETRIEVE CHAMPIONSHIP

The HPR Championship is run annually by The Kennel Club, over two days usually in November. Entry into the event is open to those dogs who have achieved a 1st or 2nd place at an Open Field Trial.

*Young dogs especially enjoy their day out.*

## FIELD TRIAL TRAINING DAYS

Many of the breed societies hold training days, sometimes called 'shotover' days, aimed at those who have an interest in field trialling but don't know what is involved, and for those with young dogs to give them a chance to run as they would in a real trial, with guns and judge, but without the eliminations that occur in a real trial. They are usually held at the beginning of the shooting season so that you have the opportunity to enter a real trial should your dog (and you!) prove to be about ready.

The aim is to give each dog at least two runs in the day, as would be the case in a field trial, and for this reason the entry is usually limited to no more than fifteen dogs; on some training days you may be lucky to get more than two runs, but don't count on it. A real Kennel Club field trial judge will be present, just as they would be in a trial; as well as judging your run, they are there to act as a trainer for the day. This is invaluable if you are a beginner, or still relatively inexperienced in trials or handling – remember that every field trial judge started out as a novice once, so they know how you feel.

In a real trial, dogs can be eliminated for various transgressions (to be found in the KC 'J'(E) regulations governing field trials and working tests – see Appendix) including unsteadiness, running in or chasing, missing game, as well as others. Normally, were your dog to commit one of these faults you would be asked by the judge to 'pick up' and that would be the end of your time in the trial, but at the training day, the judge would merely advise you of the fault, and that you would have been eliminated, but then allow you to continue until the allotted time has elapsed.

At the end of a run, the judges will be happy to give their critique on both the performance of your dog and of you, the handler. They will go through the run with you, pointing out where you might have done better as a handler, if you missed ground, where it was missed, and why. The dog may have missed game because you handled it in such a way that it ended up on the wrong side of the wind with no hope of scenting the game. The judge has the experience to be able to see these things, and to articulate them to you to learn from. Even experienced handlers make mistakes, and often it is because they are so concentrated on watching the dog that they

miss the bigger picture, which the judge has the luxury of being better placed to observe.

## FIELD TRIAL JUDGING

Field trials are officiated by two judges, one of whom must be a Kennel Club 'A' panel judge, the other either another 'A' panel, 'B' panel or so-called non-panel (NP) judge, depending on the stake being run. The function of the judge is to interpret the dog's run in terms of the field trial regulations, and to assess the performance of the dog on the day. The judges work as a team, so each will make their own individual assessment of performance, but they may confer with each other when a critical decision has to be made. The assessment of the run is recorded in a book that each carries, either as a grade or

*At a training day you are not eliminated for transgressions.*

as a numerical mark, depending on the system the judge happens to be using. They will also make a note of points and retrieves to keep a tally on what the dog has done.

Judges, as you would expect, are highly experienced not only at judging, but also in field trials as competitors – each judge will have years of experience in both. When starting out, the prospective judge has to be invited to judge by a breed society licensed to hold field trials. The societies usually have a set of minimum criteria that the prospective judge must fulfil before being considered to judge for them; this will certainly include many years of field trial experience and to have won a number of field trial awards, experience of HPR work in the shooting field, as well as other criteria, which may include judging at working tests.

Usually the learner judge is first invited to judge a spring pointing test, where the first introduction in how to assess a dog's performance from a judging perspective will take place, working with an 'A' panel judge who will act as mentor for the day, as well as the senior judge at the event. After spring pointing, the working test season carries on throughout the summer, providing the prospective judge with further judging appointments. In October, the Hunt, Point, Retrieve Field Trial Association (HPRFTA) holds a training event for learner judges where judging techniques, marking schemes, performance are learned while working with a number of dogs in the shooting field.

A problem for the aspiring judge is how to get the first appointments. A judge is invited by a society to judge an event for them, and it is not the done thing to ask for appointments (the Kennel Club regulations prohibit this anyway). The first appointments usually come from the breed society to which the learner judge belongs and is most closely associated with. When the first appointment has been completed, the learner or NP judge will be allocated a judge's number by the Kennel Club, which must subsequently be published alongside the judge's name on the field trial programme.

Once on the ladder, the NP judge must judge at least four trials under four different 'A' panel judges over a minimum of three years, when an application to join the 'B' panel can be made. The 'A' panel judge provides a written assessment of the 'B' panel or NP judge (whichever happens to be the co-judge for the day) to the Kennel Club, and these assessments are taken into consideration when deciding whether a judge may be admitted to a panel.

To become an 'A' panel judge will require the 'B' panel judge to judge a further six trials under five different 'A' panel judges, with at least one Open stake. In all cases, the applicant must be able to demonstrate that they have substantially increased their field trial experience as a competitor.

Every field trial judge is expected to be fully conversant with the latest 'J' regulations that govern field trials: they do change from year to year. The Kennel Club introduced a system in 2007 whereby presenters approved by the KC deliver prepared presentations on the current regulations, followed by a written test in order to provide a common base of up-to-date knowledge.

# Appendix

# Kennel Club 'J' Regulations

The following excerpts from the Kennel Club regulations are reproduced with permission. They relate to the regulations for 2007–8, and as they are revised every year it is important to have an up-to-date copy. The Kennel Club produces a handy version in a waterproof cover, which can be obtained from them for a nominal charge.

## J(A)
### THE MANAGEMENT, CONDUCT AND JUDGING OF FIELD TRIALS

### 1. General

a. A field trial should be run as nearly as possible to an ordinary day's shooting.

b. All competitors, judges and officials must be present when the secretary or chief steward has announced the trial has commenced or when the trial is deemed to have commenced.

c. The chief steward should liaise closely with the steward of the beat who will have planned which ground is to be used for the trial. He or she should, where necessary, welcome all on behalf of the society and introduce the host, steward of the beat, judges, guns and other officials. The chief steward, moreover, should explain the outline of the day, with instructions about transport, lunch, toilets and other arrangements. The chief steward should also issue warnings on safety.

d. At the end of the day, the chief steward should ensure that the host, guns, judges and officials are properly thanked.

e. Dogs must not wear any form of collar when under the orders of the judges except for identification where necessary.

f. Dogs must be excluded from further participation in the stake if they have committed an 'eliminating fault'. The judges may also discard dogs for 'major faults'. Where a dog is eliminated for 'hard mouth' all the judges must have examined the injured game before the dog is discarded. The handler shall also be given the opportunity of examining the game in the presence of the judges, but the decision of the judges is final.

### 2. Water tests

a. A water test requires a dog to enter water readily and swim to the satisfaction of the judges.

b. If a separate water test is included as part of a stake, all dogs placed in the awards must have passed this test.

c. A handler is not entitled to ask for a shot to be fired.

Where a special water test is conducted for part qualification for the title of field trial champion (in accordance with the provisions of Kennel Club Regulations for entries in the Stud Book, Champions, and Warrants, paragraphs K2.c(3), K2.c(6) and K2.c.(8)), it must be held between 1 September and 1 April inclusive.

## 3. Judging

a. The task of the judges is to find the dog which, on the day, pleases them most by the quality of its work from the shooting point of view. They must, therefore, take natural game-finding to be of the first importance in field trials.

    A judge must also have a very good working knowledge of the breed or breeds under trial and have the interest and future of the breed or breeds at heart, since final placings may influence breeding plans and so determine the course of breed development.

b. No judge should accept an invitation to judge a trial, and no competitor should enter a trial, unless they are fully conversant with the current Field Trial Regulations.

    The chief steward of a field trial should ensure that each of the judges at a field trial has a copy of the current Field Trial Regulations.

c. Judges are responsible for the proper conduct of the trial in accordance with Kennel Club Rules and Field Trial Regulations. Judges are also expected to maintain and abide by the highest standards in accordance with the appropriate Codes of Best Practice as published from time to time.

d. All judges, chief stewards and others responsible for the organisation of the trial should be courteous and co-operative with the host and steward of the beat and fall in with their arrangements to achieve the best result possible in an atmosphere of friendliness and confidence.

e. At the start of the day, the judges should be introduced to each other and decide their positions in the line which will remain the same throughout the body of the stake. The judges should brief the guns and handlers and if, at any time, conditions force them to depart from the arrangements they have set out the chief steward should be informed so that he or she can advise the competitors, guns and others affected.

f. Judges should also make themselves aware of any special prizes which are to be awarded in the stake.

g. Judges should ask the steward of the beat what the game position is likely to be and regulate the amount of work or number of retrieves for each dog accordingly. At driven trials judges should, after consultation with the steward of the beat, ensure that dogs sitting at a drive are positioned as to have the best opportunity to retrieve runners or wounded game during the drive only when it is practical to do so (they should also, however, be mindful of Regulation J(A)4.b). They should moreover satisfy themselves that arrangements have been made for the collection of dead or wounded game not gathered by the competing dogs and where necessary its humane despatch.

h. Judges should be careful for the safety of dogs and should not require them to negotiate hazards such as dangerous barbed wire fences, ice on ponds, unsupervised roadways or walls with high drops. Whilst judges should take reasonable precautions for the safety of competing dogs, it is also the duty of the handler to satisfy himself or herself that their dog is suitably trained, physically fit and prepared to undertake the work allocated by the judges before directing it to carry out the task specified.

i. A higher standard of work is expected in stakes which carry a qualification for the title of Field Trial Champion.

j. All judges must be satisfied that the conditions at the Stake were such as to enable the dogs to be satisfactorily tested. If there was insufficient game the stake must be considered void and must be reported to The Kennel Club within 14 days.

k. It is the duty of the judges to give dogs every opportunity to work well by seeing that conditions are, as far as possible, in their favour. In all trials the work of the dog is much affected by the way the handler behaves.

Noisy handling, however occasioned, is a major fault. A good handler will appear to do little but watch his dog while maintaining at all times perfect control over it.

l. Judges should keep their opinions strictly to themselves and act on what happens on the day or days of the trial at which they are judging, forgetting past performance.

m. At the end of each retrieve or run, judges are advised to place each dog in a category such as A or B (+ or -) according to the work done. Such gradings may, quite properly, be supplemented on occasion by additional notation for reference purposes when judges are going through their books. It is, however, imperative to appreciate that gradings must never be retrospectively adjusted. Neither should there ever be any attempt to sum sequences of grades to produce a single letter grading of a dog. When all dogs have been seen by a judge, or judges, they will wish to confer to determine which dogs they wish to discard or retain; it is vitally important for judges to make short notes of each dog's work. judges should never expect to be able to trust to memory.

n. Judges on the A Panel and the B Panel must submit assessments of B Panel or non-panel judges, as appropriate, with whom they officiate. All evaluation forms to be received by The Kennel Club within 30 days of the trial.

## 4. For all sub-groups required to retrieve

a. A dog should be steady to shot and fall of game and should retrieve tenderly to hand on command. Handlers shall not send their dog until directed by the judge.

b. Judges at open stakes and championships should ask their guns not to shoot directly over a dog when it is already out working on a retrieve. In other stakes, judges should ask their guns not to shoot when a dog is already out working on a retrieve unless by so doing they are certain there would be no chance of distracting the dog from its task.

c. All wounded game should, where possible, be gathered and despatched immediately. Unless exceptional circumstances prevail then wounded game should always be tried for before dead game. If game cannot be gathered, the judge must depute this task to the official handler and dog appointed for this purpose.

d. If game is shot very close to a dog which would make a retrieve of no value, the retrieve may be offered to a dog under another judge. During the first round of the stake dogs should, whenever possible, have the opportunity to pick game shot by their own guns.

e. Handlers should be instructed where to try from and be given reasonable directions as to where the game fell. Whilst dogs are retrieving, judges should not use their stick or any other aid as a marker to show the precise whereabouts of shot game or the fall area. If the dogs tried fail to complete the retrieve the judges should search the area of fall and, if they find the game, the dogs tried, save in exceptional circumstances, will be eliminated. However, should a dog or dogs prove to have been tried in the wrong area they should not be so penalised.

f. Good marking is essential in a retrieving dog as it should not disturb ground unnecessarily. Judges should give full credit to a dog which goes straight to the fall and gets on with the job. Similarly, the ability to take the line of a hare, wounded rabbit or bird should be credited.

g. A good retrieve will include a quick and unfussy pick-up followed by a fast return. The handler should not have to snatch or drag game from the dog's mouth. Whilst judges should not penalise a dog too heavily for putting game down to get a firmer grip, they must never, however, condone sloppy retrieving.

A good game-finding dog should not rely on the handler to find the game. It should, however, be obedient and respond to its handler's signals where necessary.

Dogs showing game-finding ability and initiative when hunting and retrieving should be placed above those which have to be handled to their game. Usually, the best dog seems to require the least handling. It appears to have an instinctive knowledge of direction and makes a difficult find look simple and easy.

h.  If a dog is performing indifferently on a runner, it must be called up promptly. If more dogs are tried on the runner, the work of all these dogs must be assessed in relation to the order in which they are tried. The handlers of the second and subsequent dogs down may be allowed to take their dogs towards the fall, as may the handler of the first dog if it has not had a chance to mark the game. Game picked by the second or a subsequent dog constitutes an 'eye wipe'. Dogs which have had their eyes wiped during the body of the stake, however it may have occurred, will be discarded. All eye wipes should be treated on their merits.

If the first dog sent shows ability by acknowledging the fall and making a workmanlike job of the line or the area, it need not automatically be barred from the awards by failing to produce the game provided that the game is not collected by another dog tried by the judges, or by the judges themselves, when searching the area which they directed the handler to search. Moreover, there will be occasions when circumstances make it impossible to send a dog promptly. If this happens and a significant delay ensues, a dog disadvantaged in this way should not be penalised as a first dog down.

i.  All game should be examined for signs of hard mouth. A hard-mouthed dog seldom gives visible evidence of hardness. The dog will simply crush in one or both sides of the ribs. Visible inspection and blowing up the feathers on a bird will not disclose the damage, digital examination is imperative.

Place the game on the palm of the hand, breast upwards, head forward, and feel the ribs with fingers and thumb. They should be round and firm. If they are caved in or flat this may be evidence of hard mouth. Be sure the game reaches the co-judges for examination.

Judges should always satisfy themselves that the damage done has been caused by the dog, not by the shot or fall. Judges, for instance, must be clear about the difference between damage to the ribcage caused by shot and the quite distinctive damage caused by a dog.

Handlers must be given the opportunity of inspecting the damaged game in the presence of the judges, but the decision of the judges is final.

A sure sign of good mouth is a dog bringing in live game whose head is up and eye bright. Superficial damage, if any, in this case can be ignored. At times, the rump of a strong runner may be gashed and look ugly. Care should be taken here, as it may be the result of a difficult capture or lack of experience in mastering a strong runner by a young dog.

There should be no hesitation or sentiment with hard mouth. The dog must be eliminated.

j.  Only game shot by the guns during the trial should be used for dogs to retrieve whilst they are under the direction of the judges. Handlers may be required to use their dogs to look for game after the trial at the request of the keeper. Practicing with cold game on the trial ground is forbidden.

# J(E)
# BREEDS WHICH HUNT, POINT AND RETRIEVE

## 1. Basic requirements

Dogs shall be required to quarter ground systematically in search of quarry (hereafter game), to point game, to flush on command, to be steady to flush, shot and fall, and to retrieve tenderly to hand on command.

Any dog which does not fulfil the basic requirements shall not receive an award or a Certificate of Merit.

## 2. Number of runners

To qualify for entry in the Kennel Club Stud Book, the number of runners permitted in stakes is:

a. Open stakes: maximum 16, minimum 10.
b. Other stakes: maximum 16, minimum 8.
c. Championship - no maximum number

## 3. The trial should run as nearly as possible to an ordinary day's rough shooting for a small party of guns, numbering not more than 4 in total.

## 4. Competing

Dogs shall be run singly in order of the draw under two judges judging as a pair. A dog, unless discarded must have been tried at least twice in the line, before it may receive an award or certificate of merit.

## 5. Credit points

Systematically quartering with stamina pace and style.

Hunting with drive and purpose.
Good marking.
Style on point and production.
Quiet handling.
Dropping to wing.
Good water work.

Speed and efficiency in retrieving.

## 6. Eliminating faults

Hard mouth.
Whining or barking.
Flushing up wind.
Out of control.
Unsteadiness.
Running in or chasing.

Failure to hunt or point.
Blinking a point.
Changing game whilst retrieving.
Being eye wiped.
Picking wrong retrieve.
Refusal to retrieve or swim.
Missing game on the beat
Failure to retrieve to hand.
(excluding hare and snipe).
Without merit.

## 7. Major faults

Poor ground treatment.
Stickiness on point.
Persistent false pointing.
Disturbing ground
Not stopping to flush down wind.
Noisy handling
Not acknowledging game going away
Catching unwounded game.
Failing to find dead or wounded game (subject to J(A)4.h.).

## 8. Judges should define the beat to be worked. As much discretion as practical should be left to the handler as to how to work the ground.

## 9. Judges must judge as a pair, but record their assessments independently having established the categories to be marked. They should see as much work as possible from every dog, particularly those which impress most favourably, and assess this work carefully in every aspect. Judges should remember that the main work of a dog which hunts, points and retrieves is to find game, and present it to the guns so that they have a good chance of a reasonable shot. Particular note should be taken of the following:-

a. **Game finding ability.** This is of the highest importance. The judge must assess game finding by observing the way the dog works its beat with regard to the wind, covers all likely game holding pockets and responds to scent generally, and also by its drive and sense of purpose.

b. **Ground treatment.** In all stakes it is highly desirable that all dogs be worked into the wind wherever possible. Dogs should quarter the beat systematically and with purpose, regulating their pace to suit the type of ground and cover.

If a dog flushes game upwind it should be discarded, but if it is working downwind and flushes or runs sideways into game having had no chance to wind it, these do not constitute eliminating faults. However, the dog should always acknowledge game so flushed and stop.

c. **Pointing.** Credit will be given to the dog that acknowledges game scent positively, draws in deliberately, points staunchly, flushes only on command and is subsequently steady. Persistent, false or unproductive pointing is a major fault. False pointing may be recognised by the dog leaving its point and immediately showing no further interest in the scent that apparently brought it on point. Unproductive pointing is where the dog points residual scent. Less experienced dogs tend to persist on such unproductive points, thereby wasting time, whereas a more experienced dog will recognise this residual scent for what it is and quickly resume hunting. If, when pointing game, a dog blinks by leaving the point and continues hunting that dog must be eliminated.

d. **Retrieving.** All retrieves should be completed as quickly as possible so that the progress of the Trial is not interrupted unduly.

e. **Style.** Before final assessments of the work are made, judges should consider the style of the dogs. Credit should be given to a dog which embraces grace of movement, stylishness when pointing and retrieving and which shows keenness and competence in what it is doing. Judges should recognise that each breed within the Hunt, Point and Retrieve sub-group has its own individual style, and they should acquaint themselves with these differences.

## J(G)
## KENNEL CLUB REGULATIONS FOR GUNDOG WORKING TESTS

These Regulations should be read alongside and assume a familiarity with, Kennel Club Field Trial Regulations. A copy of these Regulations must be available at all Gundog Working Tests (GWTs.)

### 1. Introduction

a. GWTs are competitions which, by artificially simulating shooting day conditions, seek to assess, without game being shot, the working abilities of the various breeds of Gundog.

b. No title used to describe the winners of GWTs will be associated with such competition which is best understood as a means to an end rather than an end in itself.

c. The Kennel Club authorises registered societies to hold competitive gundog working tests.

d. Scurries, Pick-Ups, and other similar events are exempt, as are non-competitive club training assessments where no places are on offer. The Kennel Club also recognises that events involving unregistered dogs do sometimes take place. Such events cannot, however, be considered to be GWTs under these Regulations.

e. Application for authority to hold GWTs must be made annually to the Kennel Club and, on the form provided, applicants should indicate the number of GWTs they propose to hold in the forthcoming year.

f. Unaffiliated societies or individuals may also be accorded annual authority to organise

GWTs, subject to 1.e. above, and these must be run in accordance with the J(G) Regulations.

g. The GWT year will run from 2 February to 1 February.

h. (1) Notwithstanding the provisions of these Regulations, certain events which are not authorised by the Kennel Club may from time to time be recognised by the Board of the Kennel Club. The Board is able to grant permission for Kennel Club registered dogs to be entered for such events.

(2) A judge, competitor or promoter will not be prejudiced by participation in such unauthorised events.

## 2. Definition of Gundog Working Tests (GWT)

a. GWTs may be run for any of the three sub-groups of Gundogs recognised by the Kennel Club as detailed below:

(1) Retrievers and Irish Water Spaniels.

(2) Sporting Spaniels other than Irish Water Spaniels.

(3) Breeds which Hunt, Point and Retrieve.

b. The following classes of competition are recognised by the Kennel Club:

(1) OPEN. Open to all dogs of a specified breed or breeds, although preference may be given to dogs which have gained a place or certificate of merit at a field trial, been placed first, second or third in an open GWT, or won a Novice GWT.

(2) NOVICE. Confined to dogs which have not gained a place or certificate of merit at a field trial, been placed first, second or third in an Open GWT or first in a Novice GWT held in accordance with Kennel Club Rules and Field Trial Regulations.

(3) PUPPY. Confined to dogs of specific breed or breeds less than eighteen months of age on the date of the test.

(4) UNCLASSIFIED. Open to all dogs of a specified breed or breeds, but may be restricted by conditions as determined by the society. To include water and team tests. A water test can include dogs of any sub-group competing together. However, if dogs of more than one sub-group are competing as a team, each sub-group will compete and be judged in accordance with the Kennel Club Gundog Working Test Regulations relating to that group.

## 3. Organisation of Gundog Working Tests

a. The organisation shall agree to hold and conduct the tests within the Rules and Regulations of the Kennel Club.

b. Control of dogs. The owner, competitor, handler or other person in charge of a dog at Kennel Club authorised events must, at all times, ensure that the dog is kept under proper control whilst at the venue including its environs, car and caravan parks and approaches.

c. GWTs should be organised by a person or persons with experience of dog work under shooting field conditions. Each dog or team of dogs should have, as near as possible, an equal opportunity with any variability in circumstances, as far as possible, minimised.

d. The organisers of GWTs will try, wherever possible, to simulate the circumstances of a shooting day. They must also ensure the tests are designed to further good Gundog work, and not inhibit dogs from marking or showing natural working ability. It is important, for instance, that guns and dummy throwers are positioned with such considerations in mind.

e. The organisers must ensure that competitors are aware of the initial running order.

f. Final decisions regarding the acceptability of tests lie with the judge or judges.

g. Only dummies acceptable to the judges, will be used for retrieves in GWTs.

h. When dummies are thrown in association with gunfire in retrieving tests, the shot must always precede the thrown dummy and the gun should be positioned a plausible distance from the retrieve. With unseen retrieves gunfire is optional.

i.  A dog, when retrieving, must not be required to pass too close to another retrieve.

j.  Organisers and judges must be careful for the safety of dogs and must not require them to negotiate dangerous obstacles. Whilst judges should take reasonable precautions for the safety of competing dogs, it is the duty of the handler to satisfy himself or herself that the dog is suitably trained, physically fit and prepared to undertake the work allocated by the judges before directing his or her dog to undertake the allotted task.

## 4. Conduct of Gundog Working Tests

a.  The organisers must ensure all competitors and judges are informed that the event is being held under Kennel Club Rules and Field Trial Regulations.

b.  The Code of Conduct expected at GWTs is the same as that for Field Trials.

c.  Those taking part in GWTs shall not openly impugn the decision of the judges or criticise the host, ground, or helpers. Any cases of alleged misconduct must be reported to the Kennel Club in accordance with Regulation J13 (Fraudulent and Discreditable Conduct at Trials). In particular the provisions of Field Trial Regulations J11 (Objections), J12 (Disqualification and Forfeit of Awards) and J14 (Penalties) shall apply.

d.  All dogs must be registered with the Kennel Club. Each dog to be of a breed included within the relevant sub-group as previously defined.

e.  The organisers have the power to exclude dogs from the competition and will have the right to refuse an entry.

f.  The organisers may restrict the numbers in a GWT, in which case the right to compete shall be decided by ballot.

g.  All judges must have experience of dog-work under shooting field conditions.

h.  In an Open GWT, each sub-group must have at least one Kennel Club Field Trial Panel Judge officiating.

i.  All handlers must carry out the instructions of the judges. The judges are empowered to remove from the test any dog whose handler does not follow their instructions or whose handler wilfully interferes with another competitor or his dog.

j.  No person attending a GWT may allow a bitch in season to be on the test ground or foul any ground to be used by competing dogs.

k.  If, after consultation with the judges, members of the committee present consider a dog unfit to compete by reason of contagious disease or physical condition such a dog shall be required to be removed immediately from the ground. Any such case is liable to be reported to the Kennel Club.

l.  No dog shall wear a collar whilst competing.

m.  No person shall carry out punitive correction or harsh handling at a GWT.

n.  No competitor may withdraw their dog and leave the GWT ground without informing the chief steward.

## 5. Judging

a.  Judges must agree a common scoring system. All competitors should be informed of the scoring system at the commencement of a GWT. But, whatever the system adopted, failure to complete an individual test will result in a mark of zero. A multiple retrieve constitutes one test. If a dog fails or commits a serious fault in any part of a multiple exercise this will result in a mark of zero for that exercise.

b.  GWTs will typically be judged on a points system with individual tests marked out of 20 though, on occasion, when their organisation is more akin to that of a field trial, letter gradings may be used.

c.  Judges must ensure that spectators are a reasonable distance from competitors in line.

d. Judges should give dogs every opportunity to work well by seeing that conditions are, as far as possible, in their favour. They will be looking for dogs, which need the least handling and please them most from a shooting point of view.

e. In all retrieving breeds good marking is essential with a quick pick-up and a fast return. Judges will not penalise a dog too heavily for putting down a retrieve to get a firmer grip, but this must not be confused with sloppy retrieving.

f. Any serious fault or failure in an individual test or tests will disqualify a dog from gaining an individual award and may lead to elimination. In team tests, however, one dog's serious fault or failure will not disqualify a team from the awards. If two or more teams finish on equal points a run-off will be necessary to determine the result.

g. The judges are empowered to withhold any prize or award if in their opinion competing dogs have not shown sufficient merit.

## 6. Instructions for specific sub-group tests

a. **Retrievers.**

(1) At the start of a GWT, judges must ensure they have the correct dogs in the line, lowest number placed on the right.

(2) A Retriever must be steady to shot and fall and must retrieve only on command. Also, whenever possible, all dogs should be tested at a simulated drive, walking up and in water. A dog must walk steadily at heel.

(3) Good marking is essential with a quick pick-up and a fast return. Dogs should be credited for showing marking ability and initiative.

(4) If a dog fails a retrieve in the run-offs, it may still feature in the awards. \

(5) **Credit points.**

Natural marking and hunting ability.

Quickness in gathering retrieve and delivery.
Nose.
Drive and style.
Quiet handling.
Control.

(6) **Serious faults.**

Refusing to retrieve.
Whining or barking.
Running in or chasing.
Out of control.
Failing to enter water.
Changing retrieve.
Poor heel work.

b. **Spaniels**

(1) At the start of a GWT, judges must ensure they have the correct dogs in the line. Dogs must be run either singly or in pairs, with the lowest number on the right.

(2) A Spaniel's primary task is to find game and flush within range of the handler. In GWTs it should at all times work within that range and demonstrate thorough ground treatment. The direction of the wind has a considerable influence on the way a dog works its ground. With a head-wind the dog should quarter the ground systematically, making good all likely game-holding cover yet keeping within gunshot distance. With a following wind, the dog will often want to pull well out and then work back towards the handler. Judges must regulate the pace of the line to allow the dog to do this so that it can make good its ground. The judge will assess the handling ability of the dog and also its pace, style, drive, courage and the quality of its ground treatment.

(3) A Spaniel must be steady to flush, shot and fall and retrieve on command from land or water.

(4) When dummies are thrown and gunfire used, the gun and dummy thrower must

walk at the edge of the beat the dog is working in line with the handler.

(5) If a dog fails to retrieve in the run-offs, it may still feature in the awards.

(6) If live pigeons are released this must be treated as a separate exercise and not occur as part of an exercise involving a retrieve.

### (7) Credit Points.

Natural hunting ability.
Nose.
Good marking.
Drive.
Style.
Control.
Speed in gathering retrieve.
Delivery.
Quiet handling.

### (8) Serious Faults.

Refusing to retrieve.
Whining or barking.
Running in or chasing.
Out of control.
Failing to enter water.
Changing retrieve.

c. **Breeds which Hunt, Point and Retrieve**

(1) Organisers must be aware of the limitations and possible problems when using game for pointing exercises.

(2) Dogs should quarter the beat across the wind hunting systematically and regulating their pace to suit the ground and cover. In novice tests dogs should not normally be required to work down wind.

(3) Judges must assess quartering, by observing the way the dog works its beat in relation to the wind. They should consider how the dog covers any possible game holding pockets and its drive and style, especially as indicated by its response to the presence of scent.

(4) Retrieving tests must be set as naturally as possible and close distractions must be avoided.

(5) If a dog fails a retrieve in the run-offs, it may still feature in the awards.

(6) Dogs must be steady to shot and fall and retrieve on command.

(7) If live pigeons are released this must be treated as a separate exercise and not occur as part of an exercise involving a retrieve.

### (8) Credit Points.

Natural quartering and pointing ability.

Drive.
Style.
Good marking.
Control.
Quickness in gathering retrieve and delivery.
Quiet handling.

### (9) Serious Faults.

Refusing to retrieve.
Whining or barking.
Out of control.
Chasing.
Failing to enter water.
Changing retrieve.

# Useful Addresses

## GUNDOG SUPPLIERS

There are a great many suppliers of gundog equipment, far too many to list here individually, as a search on the Internet will quickly reveal. In case you are stuck, or don't have a connection to the Internet, contact:

Turner Richards
68H Wyrley Road
Birmingham
B6 7BN
Tel. 01213 272 500
www.turnerrichards.co.uk

Quest
Unit 24
Standish Court
Bradley Hall Trading Estate
Standish
Wigan
WN6 0XQ
Tel. 01257 425 222
www.questgundogs.co.uk

Sporting Saint
www.sportingsaint.co.uk

The game fairs are a great source of gundog equipment, with many bargains to be had, particularly at the end of the season.

## HPR TRAINING GROUPS

The following is a list of HPR gundog training groups dedicated to training your HPR for work, working tests and field trials. Although some are run by breed societies, they all welcome HPRs of any breed.

Bardantop Training Academy
Contact: C. Guest
Tel. 01299 841407

Bristol & West Working Gundog Society
Contact: C. Carpenter
Tel. 01373 462 963
www.bwwgs.org.uk

Bryantscroft Gundogs
Contact: Rory and Jane Major
Tel. 01526 388 616
www.bryantscroftgundogs.co.uk

German Shorthaired Pointer Club (GSPC)
The GSPC has a number of local branches that run weekly training courses:

> Eastern Counties Branch
> Secretary: Janice Hawkes
> Tel. 07761 337200
> Email: cabermoor@gmail.com
>
> Highland Group
> Secretary: Georgina Buchan
> Email: georgina@culdrein.co.uk
>
> Kent & Sussex HPR Training
> Contact: Suzi Burton
> Tel. 01892 861 922
>
> North West Group
> Contact: E. Kania
> Tel. 01663 750 242
>
> Scottish Group
> Secretary: Katrina Wilkinson
> Tel. 07901 551484
> Email: trinaw@hotmail.co.uk
>
> Surrey & Hampshire Branch
> Secretary: Simon Bradley
> Tel. 07834 252511
> Email: globalinterbranding@gmail.com
>
> Sussex Branch
> Chairman: Sue Parr
> Tel. 01273 386292 or 07762 146334
> Email: pruso@ntlworld.com
>
> Yorkshire Group
> Secretary: Julie Ford
> Email: GSPCYorkshire@gmail.com

Kimberley Gundogs
Professional trainer Steve Kimberley runs courses at their facility in Devon, and also runs short courses all over the country.
Contact: Steve and Coshy Kimberley

Tel. 01837 682 866
www.kimberleygundogs.com

Laochin Gundogs
Contact: Andy Cullen MBE
Tel. 07484 244499
www.laochingundogs.com

Norfolk & Suffolk HPR FT Club
Monthly training near Eye, Suffolk
Contact: C. Snelling
Tel. 01449 781 850
www.norfolk-suffolk-hpr-ftclub.co.uk

Weimaraner Association (Staffs)
Contact: P. Pickstone
Tel. 01482 657 337
www.weimaraner-association.org.uk

## BREED SOCIETIES

Bracco Italiano Club
www.bracco-italiano.co.uk

Brittany Club of Great Britain
www.brittanyclub.co.uk
German Longhaired Pointer Club
www.german-longhaired-pointer.org.uk

German Shorthaired Pointer Association
www.gspa.co.uk

German Shorthaired Pointer Club
www.gsp.org.uk

German Wire Haired Pointer Club
www.gwpclub.co.uk

Hungarian Vizsla Club
www.hungarianvizslaclub.org.uk

Hungarian Vizsla Society
www.vizsla.org.uk

Hungarian Wirehaired Vizsla Association
www.hwva.org.uk

Italian Spinone Club
www.italianspinone.co.uk

Korthals Griffon Club
www.korthalsgriffonclub.co.uk

Large Munsterlander Club
www.largemunsterlanderclub.co.uk

Slovakian Rough Haired Pointer Club
www.workingslovakianroughhaired
   pointerclub.co.uk

Weimaraner Association
www.weimaraner-association.org.uk

Weimaraner Club of Great Britain
www.weimaranerclubofgreatbritain.org.uk

## OTHER SOCIETIES

Bristol and West
www.bwwgs.org.uk

Hampshire Gundog Society
Contact: S. Enticknap
Tel. 01730 895246
www.hampshiregundogsociety.co.uk
hampshiregundogs@aol.com

The Kennel Club
www.thekennelclub.org.uk

Norfolk & Suffolk HPR Field Trial Club
www.norfolk-suffolk-hpr-ftclub.co.uk

## FURTHER READING

*Our Dogs*          www.ourdogs.co.uk

*The Field*         www. thefield.co.uk

*Sporting Gun*      www.sportinggun.co.uk

# INDEX